THY SERVANT THE HORSE

Published in 1952
by Country Life Limited
Tavistock Street London WC2
Printed in Great Britain by
Lowe & Brydone Printers Ltd
London N.W.10

Mail coach in a flood

THY
SERVANT
THE HORSE

written and illustrated by

LIONEL EDWARDS, R.I.

COUNTRY LIFE LIMITED
TAVISTOCK STREET COVENT GARDEN
LONDON WC2

Contents

Illustrations

CHAPTER ONE

Connecting Links

THE last mail coach is variously stated to have been taken off the roads in 1846–47–48. It may therefore seem somewhat out of date to write about coaching a hundred years later or even to write about horsed vehicles of any kind, since even the latter have been out of general use for close on fifty years. That, nevertheless, is the very reason for this book—our old friend ' the willing horse ' is departing. He survives only in small numbers for riding, racing, and hunting ; he is gone from the Army, except for ceremonial purposes, and almost gone from our streets and farms—especially the latter. To those few who live among horses, and the multitude who do not, it is difficult to realize the annual shrinking of our horse population, and, to a younger generation, impossible to believe the part the horse took in our daily lives in the recent past. Three score years and ten scarcely go back to the coaching age, yet connecting links are possible. For example, my own father was born in 1810 and died 1888, so he was in his prime about 1836, the high-water mark of the coaching era. He, while a medical student at Edinburgh, travelled with regularity between that city and his home at Chester. I remember little of what he told us of those days

1. Splinter bar for pair-horse vehicle, 1898.

except what was passed on to me by elder brothers, and not much of that as it was already past history and out of date, and therefore of little interest to the young, who look forward and not back.

Direct connecting links with a hundred years ago are now gone, but fifty years ago there were still quite a few survivors. I remember an old Miss Hanmer, who as a girl lived at Bodnant in the Conway Valley, telling me she used to do the latter part of her home journey from Chester by coach, as there was no railway when she was young. As the network of railways spread over the country so the coaches were taken off the road ; and, incidentally, the War Office, with a foresight not usually connected with British strategists, moved a regiment by rail on the Liverpool-Manchester Railway as early as 1840, and by 1848 had published 'Regulations relative to the conveyance of Her Majesty's Forces, their baggage and stores, by rail'. This was pretty quick work, as some of the main lines, London to Holyhead for example, were only completed in 1848.

Who was the last survivor of the coaching age ? It is usually said to have been Charles Ward, whose sons I remember had a livery business in the Brompton Road. He started coach driving at seventeen and at twenty-two drove the famous *Quicksilver*. (He died in 1899.) But S. Wilfred Smith, writing in *The Horse* (the quarterly review of the Horse and Pony Club), mentions as 'Last of the Coachmen' an old man in Pembrokeshire who had driven the London and South Wales coaches before the railway era, as being still alive in 1921 and able to recall with ease events of almost ninety years previously, so probably he was the last of that mighty race of Jehus.

In this book I have made almost no mention of military harness or vehicles as it is a subject too large to tackle in conjunction with the horse in civil life.

It has been a matter of some difficulty to get sketches of actual vehicles, although I came across no fewer than three post-chaises, one in 1910, one in 1923, and another in 1947. The last was in quite good repair, especially the upholstery. This was of damask, which is, I am told, moth-proof, and that no doubt accounts for its good condition. Coaches were less difficult. I made a drawing of the *Quicksilver* Royal Mail at Olympia in 1920, also of the *Commodore*, which was a stage coach ; and the York Mail can be seen at South Kensington Museum by anyone who takes the trouble to go there. The dormeuse, or travelling carriage, I drew at Badminton some years ago, but when I wanted to check my drawing for accuracy recently I was told the carriage had been destroyed in the blitz on Bristol, to whose Museum it had been sent on loan.

Since the advent of mechanical vehicles even the carriages of the 'nineties seem to have vanished, and I have had difficulty in finding models. In view of the mechanization of agriculture I have thought it advisable to include some specimens of farm vehicles and harness. But necessarily much of this book must be compiled with the aid of scissors and paste, and those readers who have no time to waste in flights of fancy about what took place before they were born, will have to skip pretty freely.

To me the passing of the horse is a major tragedy. I find it difficult to adjust myself to an age in which the horse has little part save as a means of pleasure, and is therefore looked on as a luxury. Moreover the entire readjustment of life necessitated by mechanical transport has produced a new type of Englishman with whom I have very little in common. Doubtless the fault is mine, but there it is.

'There is a new world coming to birth good sirs', wrote John Buchan, 'though men know it not, *and crave rather to have an older world restored.*'

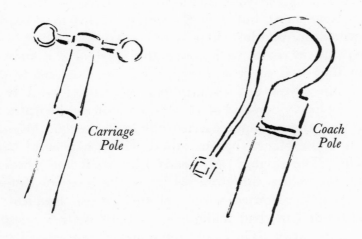

Carriage Pole

Coach Pole

2. Pole-heads for double harness.

CHAPTER TWO

The Road

IT being apparently impossible for man to walk in a straight line, even if there are no obstacles to avoid, as may be seen at any time when snow covers the ground, the earliest paths went devious ways ; and judging by some of our roads today many of these survive !

Primitive man, past and present, walks in single file. As his carrying capacity was strictly limited, he eventually devised a wheeled vehicle, which necessitated something wider than a footpath, and a more solid surface for the carriage of heavy goods. The Romans were the first to devise a proper road surface and road system. They were not content to follow winding ways, but went almost straight from place to place. They not only introduced solid foundations (many of their roads lie beneath our present ones), but they also devised a system of road drainage without which no road lasts long.

They built their roads well above the level of the surrounding swamps when they had to cross low ground, for England was full of forest and swamp. Now our country gets ever drier with improved drainage, and the heavy demand of a big population on the water supply. It is thought that the drainage carried out in the second World War, so successful in most places, has in others led to a general shrinkage of village wells. The saying ' All roads lead to Rome ' presumably commemorates the golden milestone set up in the heart of Rome, after the Romans' earliest recorded survey of their great Empire. Every legionary was trained in road making, but doubtless their prisoners of war did most of the work. They used the material nearest to hand, digging foundations, quarrying the stone, and laying their road in five or six layers, and over all a pavement where heavy traffic was used.

Thereby hangs a tale. My house stands on a Roman road, only a very short portion of which is a public road today. This old road crosses a narrow valley and runs up across a field of mine. The field must have been ploughed up by many generations of men, yet, when under grass in

3. Pair-horse Roman chariot.

a hot summer, the vegetation turns dry and brown above the road, which can then be clearly seen, while in the dip, in spite of the ox-ploughs of our ancestors and the tractors of today, the causeway can still be clearly traced ; indeed, it still stands well above the surrounding land.

But to our tale. During the war we planted this field and employed Italian prisoner-of-war labour to 'bag the taters'. The sergeant in charge of the gang could speak a little English, and one day we endeavoured to interest him in the fact that his men were the first Italian soldiers to work on the Roman road since the departure of the legions some hundreds of years ago. However, we failed to impress him—indeed, I think he understood not a word. His mind was full of one thought, and could hold no other. 'Me going home', he kept repeating.

' What part of Italy ? ' we enquired.

' Italy ? ' he replied with scorn. ' Me goin to Glasgow. Me have English wife ! '

To return to the road. Roman wheeled vehicles were more numerous than one realizes. Apart from young bloods dashing along in chariots, they had the *cisium*, a primitive, one-horse (or, I rather think, one-mule) vehicle—the forerunner of the modern gig. The Romans also had a state carriage, four-wheeled, and, of course, lots of country carts of primitive type (the *sarracum*), so that in addition to the wear of military traffic their roads got heavy use. The breakdown of the roads after the Romans left, apart from entire neglect, was chiefly due to long gaps created by water accumulating on the higher side of low-lying roads, and to the choking of the culverts that caused flooding and the breakdown of the embankments. The Imperial highways, it is said, had completely broken down by the twelfth century. The era of wheeled traffic was unfortunately over and everyone of consequence travelled on horseback. No serious attempts were made to deal with roads. Although Edward III granted a system of tolls it doesn't seem to have lasted long, or to have greatly improved the roads. Their awful state is frequently mentioned, and in that state they remained for a long time. In *Through England on a Side-saddle*, the diary of Celia Fiennes—written in the time of William and Mary—, the bad roads are frequently mentioned : ' Notably the neglected Watling Street, near Leicester, were very deep bad roads. I was near 11 hours going but 25 miles.' Celia mentions that in Lancashire ' at all crossways there are posts with hands pointing to each road, with the name of ye great town, or market towns, that it doth lead to '.

After various half-hearted attempts at road improvement no real improvement was made until the introduction of the turnpike system in 1750.

4. Roman cisium, a primitive gig.

CHAPTER THREE

Packhorses and Packways

IT seems probable that the packhorse made his first appearance in this country as early as the Bronze Age, when the pedlars (the commercial travellers of today) first went up and down the country, their pack-horses marking well-trodden tracks. Some of these tracks still exist bearing the names of the merchandise they carried, such as Rushways, Saltways, Tin or Lead ways.

There is in Northumbria, from Allendale to the sea, an old road, parts of which are still in use, but in many places it is only a grass-grown track through the heather, which never encroaches on it to any great extent, thus leaving it still clearly visible. Where the track descends into a hollow it divides in to many parallel ways, as is the habit of pack roads, the reason being that when in winter a track became too deep in mud, a fresh one was started alongside to be abandoned in turn as it became hock deep. Where it descends a very sharp decline the track becomes a watercourse. Unlike many packways, this one does not appear to be flagged with stone, as far as I could see, although I saw only one portion of it. This road, called the Leadway, goes from Nenthead to Allendale, to Emly, to Headley, and so to the docks at Newcastle—some thirty miles or so.

The export of lead has been going on since Roman times, although I think there is little direct evidence of these particular Allendale mines having been worked by Romans, but as much of the country near ' the Wall ' was so mined by them it is fairly safe to include the Leadway.

In any case there was some foreign race who centuries before Rome was built traversed our country in search of precious metals, leaving evidence of their presence in many places including Northumbria. Dr Rendall Harris has shown that the name Watling Street derives from Wat RA—the way of RA, the sun—and many other place names have Egyptian origins. This Leadway crosses the Roman road called Dere

Street—that great road that goes north by Catterick, Scotch Corner, Ebchester (in the Derwent Valley) to Whittonstall down to the Tyne, crossing at Corbridge and so on by Woodburn to Edinburgh.

Local farmers call the Leadway the Galloway Carrier Track, as ponies in the north are called Galloways, or Galls for short. The lead was carried by these Galloways on pack saddles to the docks at Newcastle, and these ponies were presumably the forerunners of the Fell and Dales ponies of today. The metal was carried loose in bags to be smelted at various places *en route*. The lead bars or ingots were then put into slotted leather bags, each pony carrying eight stone on each side. No wonder their descendants are still marvellous weight-carriers !

Travelling by pack was greatly dependant on the weather, as far as time was concerned, speed being greatly reduced in winter. The time taken in soft going, and the extra food to be carried for the Galls on each journey, meant lighter loads, slower travelling, and a greater number of ponies in use. (It is recorded that the Leadway was a pack-pony track and used through the fourteenth to eighteenth centuries.)

In early days the lead was presumably washed. Mr Charlton tells me he has seen an old lead-washing plant on the Devil's Water. It was merely a lot of water running over big trays and a pounding weight. The running water carried away everything lighter than lead : it was in fact exactly like the old Klondyke gold-washing plant. There is in Hexham-shire (a shire you may not have heard of ; I hadn't anyway !) a place called Smelting Syke and another called Smelt Mill. Both syke and mill indicate the use of water. Water was not only cheaper, but a lot more plentiful in the Allendale district, where there would be only peat, and a little timber. At any rate, presumably far back in Roman times, owing to the fuel difficulty, washing was generally used in preference to smelting.

The old Romans must have been a tougher race than the Italians of today. Although the bulk of the garrison on the Wall were foreign auxiliaries, Batavians, Tungrians, Dacians, Asturians, Thracians, Moors and Gauls, probably their officers were Romans, and they not all drawn from Northern Italy. How the unfortunate Italian from the south must have hated our northern winters ! There were two cavalry regiments stationed on the Wall, one of which is referred to on a gravestone at Hexham :

DIS MANIBVS FLAVINVS
EQ. ALAE PETR. SIGNIFER
TFR. CANDIDI AN XXV
STIP. VII. H. S.

To the Gods the Shades—FLAVINUS
Standard bearer of the Cavalry of Petriana
of the White Troop, 25 years old
and seven years service, is laid here.

Besides riding horses there must have been great numbers of animals used in chariots and still more used as pack animals. It is noticeable that the Fell ponies of today, at any rate the stallions, are a very definite type. They are inclined to be Roman-nosed, and have rather a long head. To me they suggest little Eastern blood, but descent from some northern animal, such as a Stone Age horse of foreign type as depicted by the earliest of artists (who were much more observant than most of their successors !)

The skulls of horses found at Newstead (a Roman frontier station north of the Wall, near Melrose) show several distinct types then in use. Some of the foreign auxiliaries rode a 14-hand pony whose bones suggest quite high-caste Arabians, but there were others—long, low ponies of 12-13 hands with big bone and broad skulls (Forest type) and a smaller, clean-limbed lighter pony (Celtic type). One supposes these ponies were indigenous to Britain. So perhaps our Fell pony has very ancient lineage indeed, and was the actual animal used for pack purposes by the garrison of the Wall (which is seventy-three miles long from Wallsend to Bowness and is said to have had a garrison of ten thousand men). In much later times, but still in early days of lead mining, the smelting sites were within easy reach of tidal waters, and little difficulty was experienced in shipping to London and bringing back food, etc. There was a smelting mill where Blaydon railway station now stands, four miles west of Newcastle Central, on the south side of the Tyne and on tidal waters.

Fuel was a great difficulty in early days, but Blaydon (then Ryton-on-Tyne) had coal on its doorstep. The last of the smelters to operate was one at Rookhope, where the ores from Boltsburn mine were smelted. This was also the largest producer in England, and finally closed in 1916. The other large mill was at Langley Castle, built by Greenwich Hospital

B

in 1757. It was closed in 1887. The London (Quaker) lead company, 1692-1905, had some of its mines up in the Tynehead area, a place still remote, and often inaccessible in winter. Ore was carried over thirty-five miles of wild moorland by packhorse train to Ryton, food being carried back from Newcastle, along with mining tools, clothing and other necessaries, by the same ponies.

These pack-trains remained in use until the main-road system was completed about 1826, but ponies were used in remote places far later. All the old carriers used pack-ponies instead of waggons. For example, all the fuel used in Kendal was brought in that manner, and for many years the wool from the hill farms was also brought on pony back. A pack-train was made up of some twelve to thirty ponies moving single file behind a bell mare, which had a set of bells in the middle of her collar and three small special bells on each side. Tradition has it this was for warning of their approach on narrow roads when passing would be difficult. Whether anyone still has a set of these bells I do not know, but most of the packhorse bells were smelted down when the traffic ceased.

It is now a long time since the last of the pack-trains travelled on the Leadway, but their descendants, the Fell and Dales ponies, remain with us, although sadly reduced in numbers by many causes, not the least being the number sent abroad during the first World War, which also almost extinguished that most useful animal the Welsh cob.

The Dales ponies are the small farmer's ideal horses, and there is considerable demand for them. The Fell type have, I think, a more restricted market because they are smaller. 13.2 is distinctly on the small side, but they have great weight-carrying capacity. They are more particularly the 16-stone rider's ideal heavyweight hack, for, although a bit short in front when saddled, they are active, quick walkers and unsurpassed at negotiating queer places and steep descents, and with a most good-natured temperament, suitable for both the aged and the nervous rider. In addition they make a very useful animal to put between the shafts of a governess cart, and would make nothing of pulling along the largest family with the stoutest of governesses.

The Fell and Dales breeds in these days have slightly diverged in type. The Fell stands about 13.3 hands and the Dales about 14.3, the latter being more stocky (a small-holder's ideal cart-horse). The principal sales are held in Co. Durham, while Barnard Castle and Bishop Auckland are the great breeding centres. The Dales ponies, which used to run on the hills, have become bigger animals with a strong Clydesdale cross in their make-up. Although it is usually believed that Dales and Fell ponies are separate breeds, it would appear probable that they were formerly the same animal called, west of the Pennines, Fell, and on the east, Dale ponies.

'The Packhorse,' now seen only as an inn sign, is generally depicted carrying wool. Under Roman rule the foundation of the wool trade was laid, and it was later to rise to the position of our major industry. In Tudor times the supremacy of the sheep led to cries against rural depopulation, for sheep in enclosures require little labour. Kitt's rebellion (1549) was a protest against those landlords who kept large flocks of sheep, not only on their own property, but on the common land as well.

It is probable that in the Middle Ages not only legitimate traders used the packways, but that during the nights, especially on our south and east coasts, the 'Owlers' with their pack-ponies slipped their bales of wool out of the country to continental weavers, for export of wool was forbidden except from two or three staple ports. The smugglers of later date also used pack-ponies extensively, if not the actual pack-roads; they preferred travelling by forest and moorland tracks known only to themselves. Smuggling showed a handsome dividend in those days, when, towards the end of the eighteenth century, no less than 1,425 species of goods were subject to duty! There is little doubt that many of our haunted houses owed their legend of a ghost to such a simple method of accounting for noises heard at night and occasioned by the arrival or departure of smugglers.

In this same eighteenth century the real roads were often so bad that the bulk of merchandise went by packways. Not only wool, but also coal from the Midlands, china and clay from the Potteries, and cloth from the Dales were carried in the panniers of fine strapping Lincolnshire animals . . . bearing on either side their bursting packs of merchandise to the weight of half a ton. Twelve or fourteen animals to a line would travel from the North to the Metropolis, to return with other wares of a smarter kind from the London market for the country people*.

I would not like to state definitely that no pack animals are still

*Ancient Roads of England; Jane Oliver

working in Great Britain today. For example, our otherwise mechanized army retained them, and I strongly suspect that, in civilian life, one might still see goods being carried by pack on some of our more remote mountain farms. The last I myself saw was—some thirty years ago—a string of mules (or donkeys) carrying coal to a Welsh hill farm near Colwyn Bay.

One still sees peat being carried in basket panniers in Ireland, the donkey being more often used than the pony as a pack animal. In County Fermanagh I remember seeing a woman doing her shopping with a donkey, into whose panniers went her purchases ; but more usually an ass-cart carried purchaser and purchases. I have a great regard for the ass-cart. Driven usually by old ladies, they meander over the roads of Eire, and so slow up traffic that Ireland has no need of huge advertisements saying ' Keep death off the road '. Whether one can see pack animals in the Western Highlands and Islands of Scotland today I do not know, but until fairly recently ponies were used in the Hebrides for carrying peat in creels (basket panniers) and the ponies of Barra (most southern of the Hebrides) were at one time also in great demand to drive in pony carts. They were good-looking little ponies (13 hands) said to have been crossed with Arab stallions by the Chiefs of Clan MacNeil in early days. As local roads were improved and wheeled vehicles could be used, the ponies were crossed with big, stout ponies from Uist and, unless some survive in the Island of Eriskay, adjacent to Barra, the old type is probably extinct.

The leases of some of the Skye farms conferred on the tenants the rights of foreshore. The most valuable of these was the right to gather sea-ware, for use as manure in the fields. The crofters in the neighbourhood of the farms eagerly sought the privilege of gathering sea-ware, and this was usually granted in return for labour at seed time and harvest . . . Cutting of sea-ware was done at low water during spring tides. Every available man and woman turned out with sickles to cut the golden clusters . . . As the ware was cut it was carried by ponies in creels and built into a great heap known as Rha toghar.*

Unfortunately we have not much information about the packhorse as a distinct breed. The ideal pack animal is a packhorse in miniature. He must be low to facilitate loading the pack saddle, and with strength

*Highland Ponies ; John Macdonald

he must combine great activity (more especially in modern times when pack animals are only used in hill countries). There seems no doubt, however, that the packhorse as a definite and distinct breed has died out. Most modern books on the horse never mention the breed. I have waded through quite a lot of books on the ' 'Oss ', if not quite all that Mr Jorrocks measured. You will remember he ' tuk a footrule and measured a whole yard and a half of real downright 'ard printing on the word 'Oss and they (the printers) have been at it ever since '. One book on the horse published in 1837* states that ' the horses which are still used in Devonshire, particularly in the western and southern districts, under the denomination of packhorses are a larger variety of the Exmoor and Dartmoor breeds '. The book goes on to describe a form of carriage by pack that I have not heard of elsewhere :

There are many farms in that beautiful part of England on which there is no pair of wheels. Hay, corn, straw, fuel, stone, dung, lime, etc., are carried on horseback. This was probably in early times the mode of conveyance throughout the kingdom, and has continued in these districts partly from the hilliness of the country, and more from the backwardness in all matters of improvement. Light articles such as corn, straw, faggots, etc., are carried in ' crooks ' formed of willow poles of the thickness of a scythe handle, bent as oxbows, and with one end much longer than the other. These are joined in pairs by crossbars 18 inches long, and each horse has two pairs of them slung together, so that the short end lies against the pack saddle, and the longer stand 4 or 5 feet apart, and rise some 15 or 18 inches above the horse's back. Within and between these crooks the load is piled. Dung, or sand, are carried in pots, or in strong coarse panniers slung together in the same way. At the bottom of each pot is a falling door, and at the end of the journey the trap is unlatched and the load falls out. There was also a shorter variety called ' cribs ' used when they best suited the nature of the burden to be carried.

The first cart introduced to Dartmoor was in the parish of Peter Tavey, for it is recorded that this new method of conveyance was at first looked on with such disdain, that a farmer, annoyed by the banter of his neighbours, took out his horse, turned the cart over in a turftie

*A Hundred Years of Dartmoor ; W. Crossing

(turftie was the pit from which turf had been dug), covered it with peat, and left it to rot.

Peat was not only the fuel of the farmer and his men, for there was a regular trade sending peat to neighbouring towns. Long strings of packhorses could be seen in the streets, and people buying peat in small quantities—the poorest in pennyworths. Incidentally, in the early days of the convict prison, peat was cut by the convicts for fuel before the days of the railway to Tavistock.

Recently, and quite by chance, I was shown at Buckland Filleigh a photograph of a Devon packhorse. This led to Lt.-Col. W. P. Browne lending me the minutes of a meeting held at the Castle, Exeter, on December 2, 1913 (Lord Fortescue, President) ' To promote and improve the breeding of packhorses, with a view to establishing a type of brood mare calculated to breed heavyweight riding horses ; and to compile and publish a stud book of such horses '. These minutes say :

> Stallions must have three crosses of foundation pack blood, their sires must have been pack stallions and the dam's sire and grandsire must both have been pure pack stallions. The Committee may after 1918 admit any mare in the Welsh Cob Stud Book, or any bred by Mr R. C. Monson's ' Shales ' blood.

Another meeting was held in January 1914 at which it was resolved that the following be recommended as foundation sires : King of the West and Black Prince (already dead), Buller, Lord Nelson (a Welsh cob), Findon Shales, Performer, Pride of the Dart, The Squire, Sportsman, Cottager, Triumph I and Triumph II, also known as Young Triumph. The list of names, only twelve in number, strikes me as remarkable for the ages of the ponies. The youngest is eight and the majority fourteen years and over ; evidently there were few young stallions coming on.

In 1913 the late Major A. Scott Browne started a packhorse stud at Chalhanger and the following stallions are mentioned in the estate diary : Findon Grey Shales—sold in 1916 to the Duchy of Cornwall to start a packhorse stud—Lord Nelson, Black Shales and Buller.

Major Scott Browne bred Buckland Filleigh Comet (foaled 1913), who was sold to a farmer at South Zeal, Oakhampton, and was in his old age given to Lt.-Col. W. P. Browne at Bryanston, Dorset. Here Comet served several mares and eventually died aged about twenty-seven.

5. Winter on the leadway : a pony pack-train.

Curiously enough, about twenty years ago in Wiltshire, I made a sketch of a grey stallion pony said to be a son, or grandson, of Findon Grey Shales. However, I think from the proximity of Wiltshire to Dorset, the pony was more likely a son of Comet, but definitely it was of pack-horse blood. In 1919 Major Scott Browne sold his entire packhorse stud, and as I think the Duchy of Cornwall no longer has any packhorses. I am afraid this is another breed of horse now extinct. There must be, however, still a few old people alive who could give more information than I can about them.

Incidentally Lt.-Col. Browne bred a good little mare from Filleigh Comet, a bright bay, but lacking in bone compared to Grey Shales. The stallion Buller aforementioned, was really a Welsh cob bought out of a haulier's cart by the late Major Scott Browne, and entered by him into the Packhorse Stud Book.

CHAPTER FOUR

Traffic, Transport and Travel

SEVENTEENTH CENTURY

1600   The Duke of Buckingham is supposed to have been the first man to use a coach and six in England.

1609   The duty of repairing roads was entrusted to a Royal 'Waymaker'.

1640   Stage coaches made their first appearance at this date. They carried six to eight people and were leather-curtained with a large basket slung behind. Glass was not used in these coaches until 1680.

1663   Hackney coaches for hire were first put on the streets, the first hackney rank being set up in the Strand. These coaches were two-horsed and were mostly old coaches discarded by the rich. Hackney carriages were said to be causing much inconvenience to commerce, and a Royal proclamation was issued for the purpose of suppressing them. Under licence, sedan chairs were introduced by one Sir Saunders Duncombe. They became very popular for a number of years. One of the reasons (apart from the fact that they were fashionable) was that they were easily carried through narrow and crowded streets of those days, while cumbersome hackney coaches made slow progress and shook their occupants pretty severely as they bumped over the uneven, cobble-stone streets. Hackney coaches were, of course, quite innocent of springs.

1685   Macaulay says in his *Sketch of England in 1685* 'We attribute to magnificence what was really the effect of a very disagreeable necessity. People in the time of Charles II travelled with six horses, because with a less number there was great danger of sticking in the mire'.

1668   Pepys notes, in June 1668 : 'To menders on the highway 6d'.

Apparently at this period it was usual for travellers to give alms to road-menders, and how bad the roads, or rather quagmires, must have been can be gathered from the fact that Charles II (in 1662) refers in Parliament to the mending of the ways. He begged that the Queen might enter with decency, and not find Whitehall surrounded by water.

1669   Saw the first 'flying' coach which travelled from London to Oxford in one day.

EIGHTEENTH CENTURY

1700   In this year it took a week for a vehicle to go from London to York.

1754   It was decreed by Parliament that no wheeled vehicle, unless drawn by fewer than five horses, should travel any turnpike road, unless the wheels were nine inches wide at least, under a £5 penalty.

1754   A stage coach ran between London and Manchester twice a week.
Barring accidents, it took four and a half days, but by 1815 this was reduced to thirty hours, and after the news of Waterloo to eighteen hours.

1775   There were by this time 400 stage coaches in use, according to the Annual Register.

1777   Pitt brought in a tax on male servants and a lesser tax on female domestics.

1782   Although ladies drove in a chaise their male attendants usually rode, while the manservants took the maids behind them, riding pillion, when the whole family went a journey.

1783   A tax was imposed on wagons, but this was merely an enlargement of the carriage and coach taxes introduced in 1747. The wagon tax was soon repealed. In fact taxation, very much as in modern times, was placing a stranglehold on the country's industry.

1785   Pitt brought in a tax on horses—ten shillings for saddle and carriage horses.

1796   This tax was extended to agricultural horses. These taxes adversely affected the supply of horses, but were not abolished until 1874.

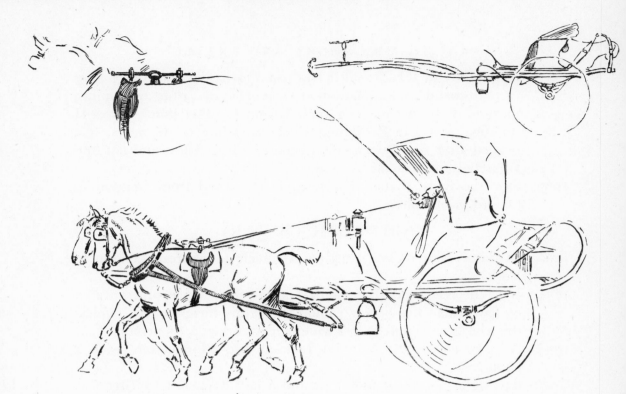

6. *The curricle*. Above left : *curricle pad ;* right : *curricle with shaft and pole.*

CARRIAGES

The eighteenth century saw the introduction of the landau, the barouche (1745) ; the cabriolet, the post-chaise* (1750), the gig (1782) and the curricle (1794).

As the curricle and its harness and method of traction was unusual, perhaps it deserves a further description. In Felton's *Carriages* (1794) the diagram shows both pole and shaft, the near horse being in shafts ; but Downman's picture shows harness only, and incidentally the animals appear on the small side compared to the vehicle, although actually this was very light.

The vehicle known as a curricle had a steel bar passing from one horse to the other over their pads ; the pole was supported from this cross-piece by a strap, or brace. The chief difference between normal double harness and curricle harness lay in the pads. These were strong and heavy, and were fitted with roller bolts on which the steel curricle

* The chariot, a closed carriage to hold two persons was, when the driver's seat was removed, often called a post-chaise

bar rested. They were of necessity both strong and heavy because at times the pole put considerable weight on them, especially downhill. On each side they had a leather loop as on a tandem pad (not shown by Downman, nor in my sketch), through which the traces passed. In the bolts on top of the pads a small steel roller was pivotted. The curricle bar rested on these rollers and was able to work freely from side to side, without friction or noise. The rollers could be raised or lowered if the horses were uneven in size, and thus kept level.

Captain Morley Knight, in his book *Hints on Driving* (1894), mentions ponies of 14 hands and upwards. These would look too small in a dog cart in single harness, but would look extremely well driven as a pair in a curricle. So perhaps Downman's proportions are not far wrong after all.

7. The britzka.

NINETEENTH CENTURY

A number of new or revised types of carriages came into use in the early nineteenth century.

1817   The dog cart.
1820   The park phaeton and the pony phaeton (beloved of George IV).
1829   The omnibus. Brought to this country, by John Shillibeer, from Paris.

8. Two travelling coaches. Left, a coach of 1794 ; right, a dormeuse of 1836.

1830. The mail coach by this time had arrived at its zenith for stability, lightness, and speed. For example, London to Exeter, a journey of 175 miles, took eighteen hours. In the very old coaches there were no roof seats, but Hogarth shows passengers precariously perched on the roof. Palmer's mail coaches began to run in 1784, and up to 1834 only three passengers were allowed to travel outside on the mails.

1834 The first hansom cab appeared—the invention of Hansom, of Hinckley, Leicestershire. This vehicle soon became popular and was improved in 1836 and again in 1873. The one-horse, four-wheeled cab, originally called, I think, a Clarence, but in modern times a growler, appeared about 1835.

1836 By this date the fastest coaches were those running between London and Brighton, 51½ miles in five and a quarter hours ; London and Manchester, 187 miles in nineteen hours ; London and Holyhead, 264 miles in twenty-six hours fifty minutes.

1839 Lord Brougham's vehicle, called after him, was first built in 1839.

The improved type with perch C-springs and under-springs first appeared in 1845. Broughams have only recently vanished from our streets.

1848   Mail and stage coaches fast disappeared from the roads with the advent of the new railways.

1880–90   The greatest improvement in shape, style, and suspension of carriages seems to have been made at about this period. Yet only some twenty years later the horsedrawn vehicle began to disappear from our roads, with the advent of mechanization.

THE GRAND TOUR

The desire for travel seems first to have overtaken the English people about 1775. Among the well-to-do The Grand Tour was the fashion, and this continued for many years.

My own father did his grand tour at a later date (about 1850) taking the whole family, nurses and all, to Italy. This was done by post-chaise and diligence with hired horses. What it cost him I have no record, but like many Englishmen of the period, he returned with some pretty bad pictures (very far from being old masters) and a distinctly depleted purse.

The scions of the great houses did the grand tour as a matter of course and took their own travelling carriages and servants, but hired the horses from place to place. The carriages, although very heavy, were roomy and commodious, able to carry much luggage in front and two servants behind. They were the last word in luxury, beautifully sprung. The floors lifted up and in the well below were carried food and wines. In an inside cupboard were carried swords or pistols according to the period in which these weapons were required, or might be required, for highwaymen, or rather brigands, were common on the continent for many years later than 1850. My mother told me that when they stopped at a posting inn at St Gothard to change horses, they were warned they might be intercepted, and she was convinced that the handsome foreigner who shared their lunch was the brigand chief, because he asked so many questions. But he presumably came to the conclusion that a family with so many children was not worth robbing.

CHAPTER FIVE

All The King's Horses

ALTHOUGH the horses used in the coaches of former days were always supplied to the Post Office on contract, the fact that their work was O.H.M.S. entitles them, I think, to be included among 'all the King's horses'. In early days, apparently, mounted couriers maintained communication between widely separated places, and as relays of horses were found necessary, stations were erected on the main roads which were called posts.

In later times, the roads having fallen into decay, these couriers made slow progress in spite of the superscription on the letters which read: 'Ride! Ride! Spur and spare not!' The so-called roads in winter had the depth and consistency of a ploughed field after rain, and it is recorded that during the Civil War the Roundheads captured 800 Royalist horses, not in battle but stuck in the mud. The couriers, or postboys, eventually achieved the distinction of being the slowest and least reliable means of conveying letters, and they were, not without reason, also suspected of tampering with the mails. Their speed was in any case a bare five miles an hour, which, even on the roads of those days, was scarcely rapid. There were, of course, coaches (cumbersome affairs with six horses to pull them through the mire) as early as 1640, but the use of coaches to carry the mail came much later.

A theatrical manager, John Palmer of Bath, first suggested the carriage of the mails by a coach drawn by four horses, contracted to the Government and guarded by a Government official, and in the *Bath Chronicle* dated July 29, 1784, the following notice was displayed:

On Monday next the experiment for the more expeditious conveyance of the mails will be made on the road from London to Bath and Bristol.

Letters are to be in the London office every evening before eight o'clock and to arrive next morning in Bath before 10 o'clock and in Bristol by 12 o'clock.

9. *Front view of the ' Commodore' road coach, Rochester and London, 1839. The coach was painted yellow and black, and could carry six inside and ten outside—including driver and guard.*

On September 16, 1784, it is recorded in the *Bath Chronicle* that the driver and guard of the mail first appeared in Royal livery and ' cut a most superior figure'.

Although Palmer's idea was at first ridiculed, the first mail coach started in 1784. The mail coaches soon caught on, and the reason for their marked success was, of course, that proprietors gained by carrying passengers in addition to their contract for carrying the mails, while the passengers on their part appreciated the increased speed, security, and, above all, punctuality of this new method of travel.

The mail coaches travelled often by night and, galloping across the map, could carry only a few passengers. The stage coaches, which travelled by day, carried a considerable load of both passengers and luggage, with perhaps greater safety, but at a much reduced speed. So coaching became a great industry, and the ' passion for the ribbons ', as the love of coaching by amateur drivers was called, was largely responsible for the increasing efficiency and the saving of time in the delivery of letters and parcels by post. It was, in fact, the beginning of postal delivery as we understand it today.

As time was all-important, it is not surprising to find that the guard's clock (carried in a locked case) was an even more significant addition to his equipment than his blunderbuss, or even the coachman's whip. The latter must at times have been used pretty freely, as all sorts and conditions of cattle found their way into the coaching stables. Only three minutes were allowed for changing horses, and this time was improved upon until forty-five seconds was reached. The *Tally-ho* Birmingham coach did a mile in 4 min. 12 sec. (London to Birmingham, 109 miles, in 7 hrs. 39 min.) Pretty good going for four horses in a laden coach !

Some idea of the magnitude of the coaching business could be gained in those days by going to St Martins-le-Grand to see more than fifty coaches leaving in quick succession for Liverpool and the North.

As a natural result of the general speeding up of the Royal Mails, racing came in, especially among the day coaches. May Day was the great day for racing between the rival coaches. A race between the Chester and Holyhead mails is recorded which led to tragic results and the imprisonment of both drivers for a considerable time.

As a check on their servants, coach proprietors employed inspectors, really professional informers, who patrolled the roads ' to prevent the coach-men from infringing the innumerable laws enacted for the regulation of their conduct '. The most common offence was ' shouldering ', that is carrying additional passengers whose names were not entered on the way-bill.

The armed guards on the mail coaches, in their red liveries, started rather badly under Mr Palmer's scheme, as they were very free in letting off their blunderbusses. However, the postal authorities soon checked these schoolboy propensities and gave the guard so much to do that he had little time to indulge in them, and a further deterrent was a £5 fine for ' firing without due cause '. The guard's first and foremost duty was the care of the mail-bags. The passengers were no concern of his, but

10. Flint-lock blunderbuss carried on the York-Newcastle coach.

whatever happened the mails must be delivered. The great storm of 1836 showed these loyal servants at their best, and there were several instances of guards appropriating the leaders of the coach and getting across country through blinding snow-storms to deliver the letters safely after incredible hardships.

The guard was paid only ten shillings a week, but his position gave him plenty of perquisites, and his uniform, a red coat, gilt buttons, blue waistcoat, and a hat with gold lace and a cockade, made him an object of much adulation, although for popularity with the fair sex it was a dead-heat between him and the coachman.

I believe the first threat to the horsed coaches was not the railways but the steam coaches—for example, Gurney's steam coach, of which Tom Hood wrote :

> *Instead of journeys people now*
> *May go upon a ' Gurney '*
> *With steam to do the horse's work . . .*

As far as I am aware the postal authorities never used these early mechanical vehicles, but with the advent of the railways the G.P.O. quickly realized their advantages, and in 1838 the mails were despatched by rail.

The passing of the coaching era ruined the coachmen, but it little

11. London horse-drawn post van, 1943.

affected the guards, who were G.P.O. servants and who merely changed from coach to railway guards. With the coming of the motor car another change in the transport of the mails took place. The first experimental motor mail van (capacity seven hundredweight) had a horse-van body and wheels. It was operated in London in 1905 by McNamara and Co., the Royal Mail and road transport contractors.

Even for longer distances the horse held his own until 1905, when the Brighton coach was superseded by a motor van. Horse-drawn red vans carrying all classes of mails were still used for many years.

Today, in mountain and moorland districts there are still a few mounted postmen. I have in recent years seen them on Exmoor and on the Welsh hills. They own their own horses and the G.P.O. pays an allowance for their use. Once, on Exmoor, I remember asking the local postman why he used his bicycle up and down a certain terrific hill, as it seemed a most unsuitable and exhausting form of progression, especially as he had a pony of his own which he used on other occasions. He replied that he was not covered by the G.P.O. in the event of accident if he used a horse. An enquiry on this point elicited that the G.P.O. considered

12. Postilion (1820-30) on a cockhorse, or trace-horse, helping a coach up a steep hill.

him on ' cycling duty ', and as such would pay workmen's compensation if he met with an accident ; but if for his own purposes he used a horse, an accident would not be regarded as ' arising out of and in the course of his employment '.

The advent of the internal combustion engine considerably altered the Post Office services, but it was not until 1919 that the Post Office became the owner of a motor transport service. Previously to that, all, or nearly all, of their transport was in the hands of contractors. Except perhaps in a few places in mountainous country with primitive roads and tracks, where their use would be difficult or uneconomic, it is the small motor van which has transformed rural postal services over the greater part of the country to an extent that would astound our ancestors.

Let us return to horse traffic, and the working of the mail by contract. In 1905 McNamara's stabled 1,300 horses, but in 1934 the Post Office had scarcely a horse-van working for them. Yet it was found that in London horse-drawn vehicles were more economical. The horsed vans in use until recently were the lineal descendants of the two-wheeled post-carts which delivered the post-bags from the General Post Office in the City to the mail coaches at their various starting points. Their use was confined to the central areas where a large number of collections have to be made in a limited mileage and over a limited period of the day—journeys which entail many stops and starts. The distance travelled per horse was about fifteen miles a day (which is a mile less than the usual journeys of the General Omnibus Company's horses, who proved themselves in the South African War of 1900 to be the most hardy, fit, and efficient animals of all Queen Victoria's four-footed servants).

One evening in 1943, in Holborn, I watched an almost endless procession of Royal Mail horsed vans, all with rubber tyres and with motor-car wheels. At first glance I thought they were converted motor vans, but on enquiry I found they were specially designed vans, built by McNamara & Co., for this particular job, just before the second World War. The horses were considerably better than those one usually sees in modern London's streets, and were, I think, mostly Irish bred.

There was apparently considerable difficulty in those days in finding horse drivers of sufficient skill and ability to drive in London traffic, and the majority of the applicants for the job were usually of an advanced age. The supply of young horses trained to traffic was also very small, and although, at ever increasing prices, horses already broken in could be purchased, they had to be acclimatized to London traffic after purchase.

The Royal Mail horses were not specially shod for London streets

13. *Back view of the ' Quicksilver ' Royal Mail coach, Devonport and London, 1835. The coach was painted red and black.*

(which I confess I should hate to drive on myself), although, of course, the horses were fitted with studs in frosty weather. The life of a set of shoes in the metropolis was four to five weeks, varying with the weather.

The development of motor transport has greatly curtailed the use of the horse, Yet history has a way of repeating itself, and, with regard to the Royal Mails, the wheel of history had taken a full turn, for the horse was until 1950 still one of His Majesty's most faithful servants.

Although the carriage of letters by coach ended somewhere about 1838 and the last mail coach was taken off in 1848, in out-of-the-way spots local coaches carried the mails at a much later date. There was a revival in the 1880's of parcel delivery by road, called the Royal Mail Parcel Coaches, and these continued to operate at any rate up to the 1914-18 War. I have a somewhat vague recollection of helping to extricate a fallen horse from a ditch on the Oxford-Abingdon road one foggy night somewhere about 1905 or 1906. It was, I think, the nearside horse of a three-horse team, presumably the London-Oxford Parcel Mail.

These night coaches carried an armed guard as well as the driver. The former sorted the letters, as the interior of the coach was lit by oil lamps. I remember thinking the guard had the best of it on bad nights. But I learn from an article on Royal Mail Parcel Coaches (which appeared in *Country Life*, December 28, 1935) that when his sorting was completed ' he was expected to take his seat beside the driver and chat with him to keep him awake '. Incidentally, I believe the motor vans of today are still called ' coaches ' by the G.P.O.

To return to an earlier age. How long did our old friend the willing horse stand up to his labours on our behalf ? The old coach horses and the omnibus horses of later date lasted about four years. The coach horses seem to have done about eighteen miles and the omnibus horses sixteen miles per day, year in year out. One would have expected the coach horses—well fed, and with a gap between their morning and evening stage—to have lasted longer than omnibus horses ; but of course they travelled much faster. On the other hand they had not the continual strain of stopping and starting on slippery streets. All sorts and conditions found their way into old coaches. The best teams naturally were reserved for coaches leaving and entering the metropolis. The worn-out and unsound animals were put into the night coaches, where kindly darkness hid their miserable appearance from the public gaze. It was doubtless a glimpse of these unfortunate beasts that led a contemporary Frenchman to call England ' a Hell for horses '. Not that all working horses died young. A canal horse called Old Billy (whose skull is in Manchester Museum) is, on the score of longevity, an easy winner for the whole equine race—for he died in 1823, aged sixty-six ! As he was always in the service of the same company his age can be verified.

Probably one of the reasons why coach horses did not last long, although they were very highly fed (their stomachs being filled to capacity) was that their housing conditions were pretty bad. The stables were usually ancient, sometimes with thatch roofs and always dark and stuffy. A manger and a hay rack ran the whole length of the stables.

Usually only bales divided the horses, to save space, and as they frequently lay down on their sides when tired, their legs must have often been trodden on by their neighbours. The old wooden mangers became the breeding ground of every equine disease, brought in by the ever changing horse population. Veterinary science was still primitive, and glanders was rife. The coaching companies lost many animals and much money through this horrible disease, which appears to have been at last stamped out in England—at any rate, I have not come across a case since the 1914-18 War. How serious this disease must have been in the old days can best be realized from the fact that at the Battle of Blenheim (1704) the French had twelve squadrons of Dragoons fighting on foot owing to the complaint.

The life of a coach horse was ever downward (as is that of most horses even today). When fresh and young the horses worked in the smart day coaches out of London ; then in mail coaches as they began their descent ; and finally in the night coaches, which used them up. Work on those nights—when a coach carried twelve in, four out, plus coachman-guard, luggage in fore and aft boot and loaded on top with more luggage, and a pig net behind full of fish and game—was very severe even on moderately sound animals, especially in winter on bad roads and behind time. The horses were severely punished, for besides the coachman's whip a ' short Tommy' (a kind of pig whip) was used on the wheelers (this whip was never seen on a day coach) ; in addition the guard would often lay on to the leaders at the same time with an ash stick, particularly up hills.

In *Old Coaching Days* by Stanley Harris, there is a maxim laid down

14. *A steam coach at Highgate—first of the threats to the horsed coach. (From a print of 1828.)*

by an old and experienced coachman, who says, ' Hit them as can work, no use to hit them as can't ! '

The exact weight of a mail or stage coach I have not yet discovered, but the celebrated *Shrewsbury Wonder*, built by Waunde in the Old Kent Road, was exceptionally light, as it weighed seventeen or eighteen hundredweight only. Night coaches were far heavier, apart from the extra weight they carried in passengers and luggage.

Although I have been unable to find when the very last of the mail coaches were taken off the road, I think it would be fairly safe to say that the last of them were the mail coaches that, horsed by stout Highland ponies, traversed the roads of Skye, the most notable being that which ran between Portree and Dunvegan in the eighteen-eighties. These coaches carried passengers as well as the mail, and that particular route was famous for its discomfort.

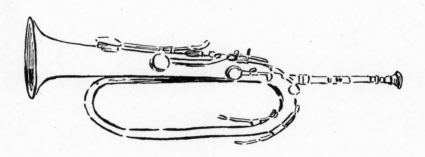

15. Key-bugle, 1830-45.

CHAPTER SIX

The Turnpikes and Toll Gates

1750   About 1750 private turnpike companies started to improve roads, previously almost entirely neglected by local parish authorities. About 1810 Macadam started really to improve and ' macadamize ' the roads. He was supported in his successful efforts by the Board of Agriculture and the Postmaster General.

1767   In 1767 a glowing testimony was penned by one Henry Horner : ' The carriage of grain, coal, merchandise, etc., is in general conducted with little more than half the number of horses formerly required.' (Not all Georgian writers quite back him up !) But the proof of the pudding is in the regularity and speed at which coaches travelled at the end of the eighteenth century and in the early nineteenth century. One of the improvements was the shortening of distances by avoiding turns and angles between towns, although by some of these straight cuts, towns such as Burford, in the Cotswolds, were left off the main road. Much more attention was also paid to gradients under the turnpike system, not only to save horseflesh, but also to save passengers walking up every steep hill beside their coaches, which many strongly objected to doing, especially in midwinter.

1819   The Postmaster General employed the famous engineer Thomas Telford to build the Holyhead road—and the Menai Straits suspension bridge became (temporarily) the wonder of the world.

Macadam and Telford covered Great Britain with a network of roads, on which, until the coming of the railways, our mail and stage coach services became the envy of other nations.

Although tolls were granted by Edward III, the real turnpike system dates only from about 1750. It eventually grew until there were often tolls as close as six or eight miles apart, and toll collectors numbered some 5,000 persons.

The effect of the turnpike system on road improvement was

16. Toll gate.

remarkable. No longer did the coachman or postilion have to
' quarter the roads '—that is to drive from side to side to avoid
deep ruts and holes.

Tolls were payable only once a day, and a vehicle could
return free up to 9 a.m. the following day. Disputes over time were
common and many toll gates displayed a clock over the door
recording official time. Public opinion against the turnpike
system at times became pretty strong, for example disaffection
broke out in Wales. The Rebeccaites rioted and gates were
demolished in great numbers. Although the receipts from tolls
increased, yet by 1836 the Government had to take in hand the
large debts of the Turnpike Trusts, and a Parliamentary committee reported adversely against the continuance of the turnpikes.
1889 Nevertheless, although tolls were largely moribund, our roads
were not even nominally free until about 1889.

The turnpike system can be roughly described as the farming out of stretches of road to individuals or companies, who improved or kept in repair existing roads, or made new ones. They made their profit by erecting gates at which they charged toll. Although some individuals made great sums of money, as time went on, and agitation increased against the number of toll gates, they formed themselves into Trusts, which invariably got into debt and had to be taken over by the Government.

The damage done by heavy vehicles was so great that the Turnpike and Highway Laws Consolidatory Act, George III, C. 40-42, allowed only wagons with not less than a nine inch breadth of wheel to be drawn by eight horses. A vehicle with a narrower gauge had to be drawn by fewer horses, and informers were even allowed to distrain on extra horses. The only exceptions were in snow, or on exceptionally steep hills, when extra trace horses were allowed. Wagons with military or naval stores were also exempt from the attentions of informers.

Even with very wide wheels these immense stage wagons, swaying and lurching along with their eight heavy draught horses, played havoc with the road surfaces—and many of these wagons crawled across the map of England, carrying not only heavy merchandise, but mixed up with it and their own luggage, people who were unable to pay for posting, or travel by coach. It must have been a picturesque sight—the eight horses wearing gaily decorated collars and 'rumbler' bells to warn other traffic of the approach of this juggernaut of the road. The driver usually rode a pony and carried a long carter's whip, which he wielded equally effectively whether mounted or on foot. Even in those days, before there existed a craze for speed, the stage wagons were considered the snails of the highway.

1947 Although you cannot travel very far on modern roads without seeing toll houses, they are not always recognized as such for the gates have gone. There was a toll house with gate on Clifton Hampden bridge until a couple of years ago. I think the toll board is still there and demands payment for a berlin, merino, whiskey, phaeton, and other long forgotten vehicles. There must be, however, more tolls in existence than I am aware of,

17. Stage wagon, c. 1807, drawn by eight horses in pairs.

as in the *Daily Mail* of March 28, 1947, the Minister of Transport asked the Highway authorities to co-operate with him in a drive to free roads and bridges.

Toll gates were naturally unpopular with most road users and the great number of them was a serious drain on contemporary pockets. The tolls varied—that for a stage coach was 1s., a pedestrian 1d., and I think the fee was 6d. for two wheel vehicles. Mail coaches were exempt from toll, and the turnpike authorities complained that the postal authorities, while insisting on good road surfaces, paid nothing towards their upkeep. This was also a reason why coach proprietors were so eager to obtain contracts to carry the mails.

The Postmaster General was quite rightly insistent on punctuality in the carriage of the mails, and to prevent excuses being made by the guards they were given a locked travelling clock whose time they could not alter. The postal authorities also compelled toll gate keepers to have the gates open for the mail to pass through. Neglect on their part meant fines of forty shillings and

upwards for delaying its passage.   Therefore the guard of the coach
always sounded his horn on approaching the gate, which flew open
at the sound : indeed all other vehicular traffic hastened to efface
itself on hearing the horn.

18. Wagoner, his pony, and one of the heavy draught horses of his team.

CHAPTER SEVEN

First Pair Out

WE are apt in these days to deplore the continual straightening and widening of our main roads for motor traffic. In particular does the horseman regret the removal of the grass verges on which, in the Highway Code, he is requested to travel. We forget, however, that these grass verges are of comparatively modern growth. In the coaching era there were few, and in many places main roads were thirty yards wide, giving ample room and temptation to mail coaches to race each other—a temptation to which they seem to have succumbed as readily as does the modern motor driver.

It should also be remembered that, despite the many drove roads (which still survive in places) on which beef on the hoof was brought down from the North, these herds, sometimes a mile long, greatly impeded fast-moving traffic when, as they were obliged to do from time to time, they emerged on to the main roads. A great width of road surface was therefore essential. Cattle which were brought by road from the wilds of the Welsh or Scottish Highlands were driven into London on Sundays to avoid undue interference with traffic, and any going out of London had to be cleared from the metropolis during the early hours of Monday morning.

In addition to the mail and stage coaches and stage wagons (eight-horsed), there was also an immense posting traffic. Not that the latter was a cheap method of travel by any means, but it was one of comparative comfort. At least the traveller was under cover and dry, which is more than can be said for our modern horse-drawn vehicles, almost the only survivor still in use being a governess cart, open to the winds of heaven. Another advantage was that the post-chaise was well sprung (almost too much so), and was therefore less tiring for long-distance travel, and in wet weather especially a thousand times better than the top of a coach. The traveller also was not crowded with perhaps most uncongenial company, and was to some extent master of his own fate,

since the post-boy was his servant for the time being.

Post-boys received no wages; they supplied their own clothing, although their master supplied board and lodging. For pay they were entirely dependent on tips. The post-boys of rival establishments often wore differently coloured hats, white or black stovepipe style with a squarish brim. In the North, red was the usual colour for their jackets, with silver braid. Waistcoats were striped, usually red and blue; the breeches were white cord; and the boots had yellow tops with an iron guard on the right leg, like those of R.H.A. drivers before mechanization. They wore only one spur, on the left leg. The neck cravat, made of white linen, was a most wondrous affair, often nearly two yards long. On state occasions in the North, blue jackets were often worn, but south of the Trent yellow jackets seem to have been the everyday wear.

Today, motoring up the Great North Road, or indeed on almost any main road, you may see a roadside hotel with the sign ' Posting House ', (The Crown at Bawtry, for example). I have also seen over a stable entrance the words ' Post-Horses ' and ' Neat Post-chaises ', but this was a few years back, and I have forgotten where it was. There is at Malvern a similar notice at the Foley Arms Hotel.

One winter, in Yorkshire, I went to a meet of the Badsworth at Barnsdale Bar, a toll house which must have once been a busy place, as five roads meet at it. To save time at the gates, tolls were paid by tickets, and the post-boy paid the money on his return journey. Travellers settled up with the boys at the end of each stage. The hotel at which the change was made usually gave the boy a meal ' on the house ' before he started home, doubtless to encourage trade.

During an election, or a race week, post-boys would make perhaps five pounds in tips, and the pound was worth twenty shillings in those

D

days. Catterick Bridge was a great cock-fighting centre, and local post-boys doubtless did well when a big match was on. Each post-boy had four horses for which he was responsible. It was a hard life for man and beast, particularly the latter. Travellers who missed the mail would heavily bribe a post-boy to overtake it at the next stage, which meant galloping most of the way.

At times the boys rode great distances. In *Old Coaching Days in Yorkshire,* by Tom Bradley, we are told that one Tommy Hutchinson rode from Easingwold to York five times in one day—130 miles. In winter they were sometimes so stiff with cold they had to be lifted from the saddle. In bad weather they wore a heavy, buff-coloured coat to the heels, with a double row of pearl buttons, not unlike the traditional coachman's overcoat of yesterday.

Some idea of the size of the posting business may be gathered from the fact that the York Tavern had always 150 post-horses in work. The boys themselves (usually boys in name only) were curious, bow-legged, wizened, wrinkled old men, given to much strong drink to keep out the cold. Their now forgotten song, *The Jolly Post-Boys,* ended with the verse:

> *He that drinks and goes to bed mellow,*
> *Lives as 'e oughter live, and dies a good fellow.*

It was a *hard* life. The horses next for use stood in their stalls with most of their harness on. The post-boy next for duty had to be ready day or night. Indeed, he slept with his one spur on, ready for the call, ' First pair out ! '

I have endeavoured, with somewhat indifferent success, to discover the cost of posting. Lord William Lennox is quoted in the *Coaching Age,* published in 1885, as having given the cost of a journey by post-chaise from London to Holyhead (264 miles) as £58 5s. 11d., as follows :

	£	s.	d.
Charge for 4 horses	38	11	6
Paid to post-boys	9	6	10
Paid tolls	9	5	1
Tips to ostlers	1	2	6

With four horses it was of course doing it *de luxe*, and obviously this journey was made in a private post-chaise with men and horses hired by the mile.

20. Post-chaise being hard driven to overtake the mail coach.

The *Bath Chronicle* (1794) gives the cost of posting at the White Lion Hotel, Bath, as : For chaise and pair, 1s. a mile ; chaise and four, 1s. 9d. a mile ; saddle horses, 4½d. a mile.

It would seem, however, that two shillings a mile was about the average hotel charge for posting with two horses, and three shillings with four horses ; threepence was the fee to a post-boy and sixpence to the ostler. The lack of dates to coincide with the text in most of the coaching books makes it difficult to discover the yearly cost of travel, but it appears to have increased to some extent at later dates.

Bob Newman of Regent Street kept perhaps the most famous posting establishment of his day (*c.* 1800). His trade was by no means beer and skittles, as the post-masters were very heavily taxed. They were charged one fourth of the gross earnings and a five guinea licence for each chaise. A gentleman travelling in his own carriage, and bound to hire post-horses, was lawful prey for post-boys, and there was tremendous competition to obtain his custom for the first stage out. Postboys were often given ten shillings by a post-master for bringing a customer to his stable, and at the next stage another seven shillings and sixpence, by which time the boy returning with the first pair could be confident he

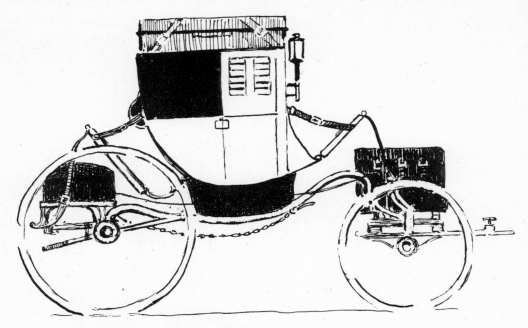

21. Travelling post-chaise with crane neck carriage, 1794.

had left his 'gent' safely in the hands of one or other rival posting establishments.

I learn that the returning post-boy usually drove home. It was presumably less tiring, although, as he sat on a cross-bar which went from the top of one of the cross springs to the opposite one and was only about four inches wide, it can scarcely have been a comfortable seat. His feet rested on the flat board which usually carried the travellers' luggage. What he did for long driving reins I have no idea, unless he kept a pair of driving reins under the seat; but there he sat with his short whip and his riding horse with an empty saddle, jogging slowly home. Incidentally, if he could pick up a fare he did so. In the larger posting establishments with say twenty-six pairs (as at the Green Man, Barnet) there were in the stable yards 'cads' who looked after post-horses, washed the chaises, called the post-boys at night, lighted the lamps, assisted to harness, and so on. The post-boys paid the cads four shillings a week. If all post-boys were out and some horses still left in, the cads rode a stage.

Presumably the word cad and the word cadger are derived from the same source. In her *Bridle Ways through History*, Lady Apsley writes: 'The man who carried the hawks and falcons was known as a cadger from the wooden structure or cadge, on which the birds perched until they were wanted by the falconer. The cadger was presumably some old

retainer or follower of the sport, hence the word cadger, a hanger on.'
According to Stanley Harris (in *Old Coaching Days*) some post-boys had
four horses—a morning pair and an afternoon pair. If four horses were
ordered, the two boys each took a pair of their own horses.

At the end of a stage, the post-boy groomed his horses, unharnessed
and fed them. He paid a shilling for their feed and twopence to the
ostler who helped him. He then went into the inn and had a free meal
and a pint of beer on the house, after which he returned with horses and
chaise to his original starting point.

Post-boys were often characters. Starting as boys they usually
remained (post) boys to the end of their days. An exception was Jockey
Norman, familiarly known to the racing public as 'postboy', he having
started life as a private postilion in the service of the Marquis of Exeter
at Stamford. Later he went to Newmarket and eventually became a
jockey. He always rode for the Marquis of Exeter and won the Derby
on Stockwell. Consequently when he attended a race meeting at Stamford he was naturally made much of by all at Burghley House. Norman
was a great trencherman (a relic of post-boy days, perhaps) and after
dinner was once asked if he would take dessert. He replied 'Thankee,
I don't mind if I do, but let's have that there beef-steak pudding back
first !' His love of the table compelled him to take long walks daily
and it required severe wasting to keep his weight down.

No doubt post-boys were a hardy race. Indeed, two sayings survive
as proof that they were so considered : 'Who ever heard of a bilious
post-boy ?' and 'Who ever saw a dead post-boy or a dead donkey ?'

Curiously enough there are not many contemporary drawings of
post-boys and chaises. There are some by Rowlandson—not very
accurate from a coachbuilder's point of view ! Sartorious, Pollard, Herring, and Garrard were all contemporary artists, and did a few pictures
containing post-chaises, but far the best of contemporary painters was
Cooper Henderson. There is much of interest in all their work. For example, Pollard usually shows bearing reins on both ride and drive horses,
but Cooper Henderson shows it on the led horse only. As far as I can
make out, when there was a bearing rein on the ridden horse it was
attached to a ' D ' in front of the saddle, at least it appears so in one of
Garrard's pictures.

The post-boy's saddle was a large and clumsy affair. There is a description of one in a memoir of the Rev. John Russell : 'Riding a hireling in an old fashioned post-boy's saddle, brass mounted and secured by a huge crupper to its rat tail.'

Posting was a great trade in its day, and quite apart from runaway couples to Gretna Green, it was a business into which romance not infrequently found its way. For example in 1774, when the banking firm of Backhouse and Company was established, Darlington contained only 444 inhabited houses. The Backhouse family were linen and worsted manufacturers, and carried on a banking business in conjunction with their regular trade before they started the Bank as a separate entity. The firm survived many local bank failures, and the story of Jonathan Backhouse thwarting an attempt to break the Bank by himself ' posting ' to London and returning with a heavy load of bullion is well known. Undismayed by the loss of a forewheel, he ' balanced ' by piling the gold at the back of the chaise, driving into Darlington on three wheels.

22. Postilion, 1830.

CHAPTER EIGHT

Fashion and the Horse

FASHIONS in everything connected with the horse have changed countless times, not only in manes and tails, but also in harness, saddlery, and even more in the liveries and stable clothes worn by those closely connected with equine matters.

To take the horse first. The hogging of manes, judging by such pictorial evidence as I can find, would appear to be a modern fashion, although the horses on the Elgin Marbles have obviously been hogged and their manes allowed to grow again to the stand-up mane that was apparently admired by both Greeks and Romans. The hogging of hunter's manes dates from about 1888 ; the plaiting of them dates from 1896, but was not common until after 1900. The plaiting of racehorses' manes is old and dates from about 1708-1720. The following famous horses are depicted with plaited manes (when with jockeys up) : Basto, by Byerley Turk ; Bay Bolton, by Grey Hartley ; and Fox, by Clumsy.

In early Georgian times the ears of both saddle and harness horses were cropped. Hunters had cropped ears, long manes, and only medium short dock tails.

Carriage horses usually had half-dock tails, but a grey pony in a phaeton (by Stubbs) has a long mane and tail. The period 1820-30 is that of the real gamecock tail, often nicked as well to ensure high carriage. By 1850 tails were long, but the fashion of 'pulling' the side hair near the dock is quite modern (and foolish). Of course there were, and still are, a few cock-tails among the cobs and also the heavy hunter types.

The Sovereign's Escort at Charles II's Coronation had their horses' manes and tails plaited with blue ribbon, but I think that, except on State occasions and at shows or sales, plaited manes were seldom seen until people started plaiting the manes of racehorses and hunters in comparatively recent times.

You may have noticed that a cart-horse got up for sale with straw and ribbon decorations has often a long ribbon hanging from the withers

23. *Nobleman's state coach in the nineties. The liveries worn by coachmen and carriage grooms were most elaborate, and included hats trimmed with ostrich*

feathers, brightly coloured frock coats trimmed with gold braid, knee breeches,
silk stockings, and silver-buckled shoes.

24. A nobleman's coachman in state livery.

end of its mane almost to the ground. A dealer in draught horses once told me that this was not only an ornament, but was also an endeavour by the seller to defeat the eye of the purchaser, as it made a leggy horse appear to stand less high off the ground ; the same idea, in fact, as the ordinary dealer's trick of placing the saddle too far back to make the horse appear to have more in front of the saddle.

The plaiting of the forelock as a charm against the evil eye is so old that it is said to go back to Borak, the horse that transported Mahomet to the Seventh Heaven.

With men's clothing it is difficult to know where to begin. Obviously liveries have evolved from the costume worn by the armed retainers of olden times. It may seem odd to start with footmen instead of stablemen, but about the first picture of what appears to me to be livery is one by Wooton (1716) of Lady Henrietta Cavendish Bentinck with a running footman in front of her horse. I should think, apart from my knowing of no other, that he must be about the last of the running footmen, whose duties must have ended as a better bred, quicker type of saddle horse came into use. The connection between the horse and the footman from then on was negligible. In Victorian times he merely sat on the box beside the coachman, opened carriage doors, carried parcels and rang bells for his mistress, and I think in any case he only took ' carriage exercise ' when his mistress had no carriage groom. Footmen were often imposing figures in winter, with their fur tippets and long coats and top hats, as they waited for their mistresses outside the more fashionable shops in the West End, in the 'nineties. Although perhaps in the establishments of the great a stud groom ruled—perhaps under a a master of the horse—the coachman was the most important personage from early days in most stables.

Early Georgian coachmen's liveries are to be seen in some of Canaletto's pictures, and the full-dress livery of a nobleman's coachman at a Coronation or other State occasion is almost exactly the same today, or at least was up to 1900, as I do not think dress or State carriages and full-dress liveries have been much used by private persons since about that date.

A contemporary tells me, however, that he remembers State carriages up to the opening of Parliament in 1914, and in particular remembers that the horses in the Austrian Ambassador's carriage fell, breaking the pole on that occasion. 'There were four or five State carriages at George V's Coronation, those of the Lords Londonderry, Lonsdale, and the Dukes of Westminster and Marlborough; and possibly the other was the Duke of Sutherland's.' I quote this from a peer who was present. That was about the end of private State carriages. Up to the end of Victoria's reign the Diplomatic Corps in London had their own State carriages. Probably handed down by one Ambassador to the next (and maintained by Messrs. Hooper) these carriages were always used when the Ambassadors presented their credentials or went to the Palace on any kind of official occasion.

25. Footman acting as carriage groom, London, 1898.

Since my own memories of equine matters start in the early 'nineties, perhaps I may enlarge on the subject from about that period. There were, of course, coachmen and coachmen. In the larger establishments there were a first and second coachman and a carriage groom. They usually wore black coat and trousers strapped underfoot, yellow striped waistcoats, top hats and cockades, double-breasted drab overcoats with livery buttons and leather gloves, of best quality, except in cold weather. In winter they wore black mackintoshes with velvet collars, and grey woollen gloves. This livery would be worn for ordinary station work or business calls; for social occasions, livery as above, but with white

*26. Groom in stable
dress, 1880-90.*

leathers and top boots. Their stable suits were grey Bedford cord, bowler hats, and buff cloth leggings.

Liveries were not always black. I remember that green, blue, and plum colour were often worn, and on State occasions coachmen's bright-coloured liveries were most elaborate : three-cornered hats with white ostrich feathers, frock coats almost any colour, with much gold braid, epaulettes, wide cuffs, knee breeches, white or flesh coloured silk stockings, silver buckled shoes, and, of course, powdered wigs. I don't remember seeing this dress later than about 1910.

The first coachman had nothing to do but drive, unless his mistress drove herself in phaeton, dog cart, or pony carriage, in which case the carriage groom accompanied her. There is a tale told in our family that my father, meeting my mother returning from a drive in the dog cart, said, ' Hullo ! Where's your groom ? '

' Oh, did I have a groom ? ' she replied.

A few minutes later, Bob, the groom, arrived, purple in the face, having been tipped out from the back seat in coming too sharply round a corner, and having run after the carriage in his top boots.

To go back to larger establishments, the job of the second coachman was to drive his master, should her ladyship want the other carriage. The second man also did a certain amount of stable work himself. Of course, if the master drove himself he also had a groom with him. In London the first footman took the place of the carriage groom as a rule, and the second coachman was seldom brought up to London for the season. In many establishments great pride was taken in the general turn-out, and sometimes the master insisted on seeing all liveries tried on. (If I remember rightly, Sandon, of London, was most sought after for liveries.)

Besides the visit to the tailor there might be a visit to the coach-builder in London to try the seating of the new carriage. Among the names of the famous carriage builders, I can only think of Hooper, Peters and Mulliner, although there were others equally well known, many of whom have become motor-body builders.

In town, swagger coachmen had a club to which only those who drove a pair or team were allowed entry. These august personages called the ordinary driver 'a one-'oss guider', and as such he was beneath their contempt. Business men in London had a working coach-man who looked after their stables and drove them to and from their offices. This man fed and cleaned his horses but usually had a stable-man to muck out and clean harness and the carriage.

In small country establishments, from about 1880 down to the advent of motor-cars, a coachman's dress would be black coat, buttons with crest or initials, top hat with or without cockade, drab breeches with boxcloth leggings, and black mackintosh in winter or, latterly, a white one.

The livery of grooms and stablemen has always been just a little different from that of coachmen, their stable suits being more often in use than livery, and therefore one usually sees them so depicted. From the 'eighties to the 'nineties their working dress was usually a waistcoat of thick buff material, with flaps to pockets and made long (the sleeves were of thinner material and usually a different colour) ; breeches of the same material, with not much shape and rather skimpy ; box-cloth gaiters, rather bell-bottomed ; and a collar of washable rubber material, worn with a made-up stock and pin, usually black or blue bird's eye, if I remember rightly. A cap of deer-stalker type was worn with stable dress. Somewhere about 1900 the working dress became pepper-and-salt Bedford cord suits with breeches cut wide, and tight at the knee, and smart leather leggings. This stable dress, now worn by second horsemen, is really quite incorrect for hunting, but modern taxation forbids top hats, frock coats with belts, white breeches and top boots, which is the proper dress for servants in the hunting field.

CHAPTER NINE

Lorinery, Harness and Horse Furniture

HARNESS, perhaps, has changed less than most other things connected with the horse. The earliest method seems to have been the yoke. A fourteenth-century illumination in *The Romance of Alexander* (Bodleian Library) shows a horse (or is it a mule ?) in breast harness, but horses in a whirlicote, or long wagon, of about the same period have cart collars much the same as those worn today. Horses in the mourning coach of Charles II appear to have breast harness, and also in some of Stubbs's pictures (his phaeton and pair for example), but by the end of the nineteenth century the collar appears to have been in universal use, and, I think, it remained so until the R.H.A. reintroduced breast harness some time after the South African war.

The fact that equitation is very much subject to the vagaries of fashion, and the different uses to which the horse has at various times been put in sport and war, have led to greater changes in saddlery than in driving harness, perhaps the most numerous changes being in bits. Bronze bits were used 1,000 B.C. (Homer). In 1900 B.C. saddle cloths were in use, but saddles (and stirrups) are of later date. The Romans used saddles in the fourth century (and it is recorded their horses had sore backs !). The terrible looking bits of medieval warfare were a dire necessity. The armour of a man and his horse weighed 163 lbs. ; his arms, saddlery and clothes, 30 lbs. Thus, a man weighing 10 stone required what was practically a modern cart horse to carry him (although slightly smaller than today's Shire horse, as is proved by contemporary horse furniture). Their riders required very powerful bits and long spurs to manoeuvre such large and clumsy beasts in close combat. Relatively powerful bits remained in use by the cavalry until in modern times the role of the horseman became more that of the scout and less of the fighting man as the continuous improvement of quick-firing weapons reduced cavalry shock tactics to a minimum.

I have often seen it stated that the present practice of wearing short (and usually dummy) spurs is because of our more humane attitude to the horse. In fact, the spur now used reached us by very slow stages. It became milder in character as horses became lighter, more active and better bred, and as succeeding generations left the heavy type of horse farther and farther behind. The shortened stirrup leathers of today also make the long spur impracticable.

Perhaps I had better hark back to the word 'lorinery'. The Worshipful Company of Loriners still flourishes and dates, I believe, back to very early times. The word means a bridle bit maker, but actually includes the making of bits, spurs, stirrups, and the like. One

27. Types of spur.
Left, *prick spur 300-100 B.C.* ; centre, *ladies' camouflaged prick spur, mid-nineteenth century* ; right, *modern hunting spur, a dummy.*

of the best known loriners was Latchford, whose name is often mentioned by Surtees and other writers. He was Loriner to King George IV, and 'letting in the Latchfords' is an expression still sometimes used, meaning to use the spurs. Although heavy bits were used for war, snaffles seem to have been more usual for sport from quite early times. The snaffle bridle on hunters, about 1775, had a peculiar throat lash, much lower down on the cheek, about where the cheek buckle is today, while the upper part of the head stall, that is the crown piece, was a very broad strip of leather. Double bridles were rare in those days, but a picture by Seymour shows an old squire riding with a very long cheeked bit about 1779. Nose bands on civilian bridles are comparatively modern. Most of the old hunting pictures depict open bridles (*vide* H. Alken's Meltonian pictures). Actually the noseband as worn now is useless, yet to us a horse looks naked without it. Fashions have changed in decoration also. In early times metal, glass, and feathers added to the panoply of the war horse. In ever lessening quantity it remained, down to our younger days, on the full dress equipment of officers' chargers with cowrie shells, metal buckles, plumes and leopard or bearskin saddlecloths over the embroidered shabracque, etc. There never was much decoration on civilian saddlery in Britain, except perhaps coloured brow-bands. Coloured brow-bands and buckled-on reins are considered the height of vulgarity today, yet buckles allow the removal of bit for cleaning, and the use of several different bits with one bridle. We are an illogical race, ruled by fashion. In the past Ripon (Yorks) was the headquarters of the spur trade, and the spur is, I think, still that city's arms. Ripon had a Spurriers Guild, whose rules were so strict that it took seven years

28. How horse-brasses are worn : ploughing match, 1935.

apprenticeship to become an independent spurrier. ' True as Ripon rowels ' was a local saying. In the days of the horse the saying was ' Carlisle for whips, York for saddles, Walsall for harness '.

When everyone wore spurs, it was a legal right for ' spur money ' to be collected in churches ' in consequence of the interruption of Divine service occasioned by the ringing of spurs of people walking and transacting business in Cathedrals '.

The earliest form of spur was a prick spur. (See Fig. 27.) This survived to, or rather re-appeared in, late Georgian and Victorian days, when ladies wore top hats with veils, and long flowing habits. The spur had to be applied through the habit ; there were no apron skirts in those days. It was a vicious little spur (I believe I still have one somewhere) and if applied at all vigorously the horse knew all about it. Whyte Melville says in *Riding Recollections* : ' the unwary wonder why . . . a lady's horse always appears to go in a lighter, livelier form than that of her male companion. " Its a woman's hand, says the admiring pedestrian." " Not a bit of it " answers the cynic, "its a woman's heel ! ".'

Civilian saddles do not lend themselves to much decoration, but some of the earlier types of ladies' saddles with three pommels had elaborate and decorative stitching and doeskin seats. Ladies' saddles have altered a lot even in my time. Today most ladies ride astride, so even modern secondhand side-saddles are difficult to dispose of. Yet if you buy a new one they will still cost you ' a packet '. Even today, or at any rate up to the second World War, the well-turned out and hard-riding ladies in the Shires still rode side-saddle—and why not ? For looks there is no comparison between the two methods.

In trade and agriculture, however, the decoration of horse furniture is still carried on, and brasses, flyers, ribbons, and so forth are often worn, especially on gala occasions. (See Fig. 28.) These brasses are of very ancient lineage and are a survival of charms against the evil eye. There are many kinds of horse brasses, face pieces, ear bosses, studs, bells, flyers—often with swinging glass in the centre—name plates, decorated housing, etc. None of these things was made commercially before 1800, but sham ones can be found today of quite modern make, I am told.

I have endeavoured to depict the difference between cart and trace harness, and recommend the art student to compare the methods of attaching them to vehicles, as well as the different sorts of harness in cart and carriage. Among the coaching illustrations, there is one of a team depicted from the driver's seat. (See Fig. 39.) In this can be studied the method of coupling up a team. Artists frequently get this wrong.

It will soon be difficult, indeed it is now, to study carriage harness. The harness room today (now usually called the tack room) contains only saddlery. If any harness is left it is a pathetic sight, although

E

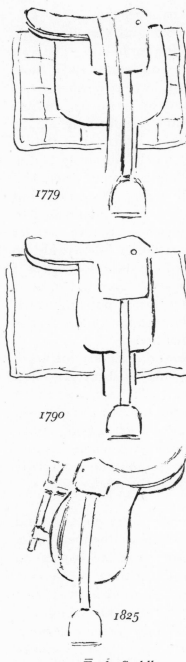

1779

1790

1825

29. *Early Saddles.*

occasionally an old servant who remembers the light of other days still keeps the unused harness in perfect condition, because he cannot bear to see once valuable stuff become the prey of moth and rust. Those few people who still do keep a harness cob or pony, always astonish me because they take so little interest in their harness. Yet it takes a lot of time, trouble, and money to make good harness, and many people treat it as if it were of no particular value. It is costly enough to buy, too. The single harness (cob or pony size) which most people buy today is usually sold at about fifteen to twenty guineas a set. Brown harness with white metal, which is many pounds dearer than that of forty years ago, seems the most popular at the moment, and the local saddler and harness-makers have still often more orders than they can supply. A brown saddler, as he is called, makes saddles, and a harness-maker makes harness ; but in small country establishments the same man makes both, and these country craftsmen, being experts at their trade, sooner or later drift to London and other centres, being in great demand by the big firms who deal in harness and saddlery and other leather goods.

Apprenticeship to the saddlery trade lasts seven years, and then come five years as an improver. I believe there is a shortage of apprentices in these days owing to the high wages unskilled labour can earn. I heard this being discussed by two saddlers the other day, and apparently the idea has been mooted that to encourage apprenticeship a subsidy should be paid by the Government

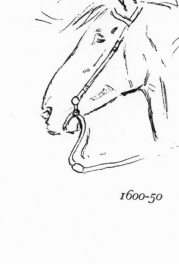

1600-50

1775
Hunter with cropped ears
and wide crown-piece to bridle.

1823
Hunter :
note position of throat-lash.

1933
Hunter with double bridle.

30. *Bits and Bridles.*

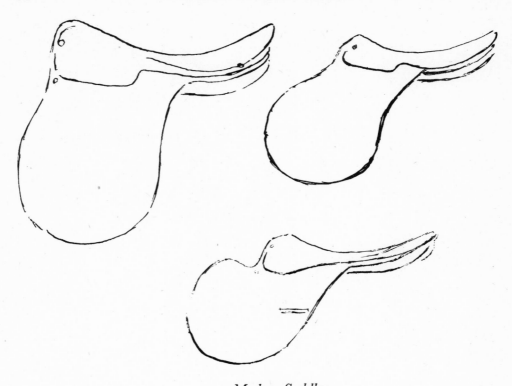

31. Modern Saddles.

Top left, *hunting saddle ;* top right, *hunting and show-jumping (forward seat) saddle ;*
below, *flat-racing saddle.*

to bring their pay more or less into line with that of other trades.

As the basis of harness is good leather, it is not without interest to learn how it is made. In some ways modern leather is an improvement on the old, for there are now no hides damaged by the bot fly. Secondly, the modern slaughterman seems more careful not to slash the hide about than his predecessor. Whether the tanning is as good is perhaps open to question.

In these days most of the leather used by saddle and harness-makers is of the eight-weeks tannage variety. The manufacture—that is tanning and currying leather—is not usually the work of one firm, but two. The tanner tans, and the currier curries. The present method takes about eight weeks. It is done with paraffin wax—how, I don't know. The old, and many people say the better, process took about twelve months and

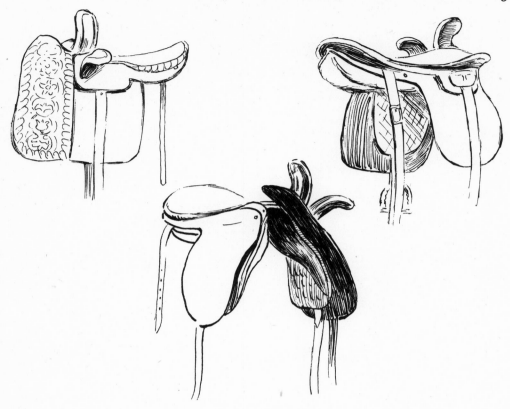

32. Side Saddles.
Top left, *1860 ;* top right, *1872 ;* below, *French 'cut back ', 1890.*

the leather was treated with cod oil and dubbin. When the latter had sunk in, the leather received further applications until ready for the saddler. Of long tannage by oak bark it was, and is, probably the best leather obtainable. Leather is bought by weight and it is not quite unknown for it to contain a lead solution to add to the weight.

The seat of the saddle is usually made of pigskin, but the flaps are usually of butt leather. Stirrup leather butts are differently dressed. Their chief essential is that they must be without a flaw. Chrome leather stirrup leathers will usually wear out two of another sort. Saddle trees are made at Walsall, as are most of the metal buckles, etc., of which there is a shortage at the moment. In the days of steel bits (still the best) many of these were made on private hand forges at the loriner's

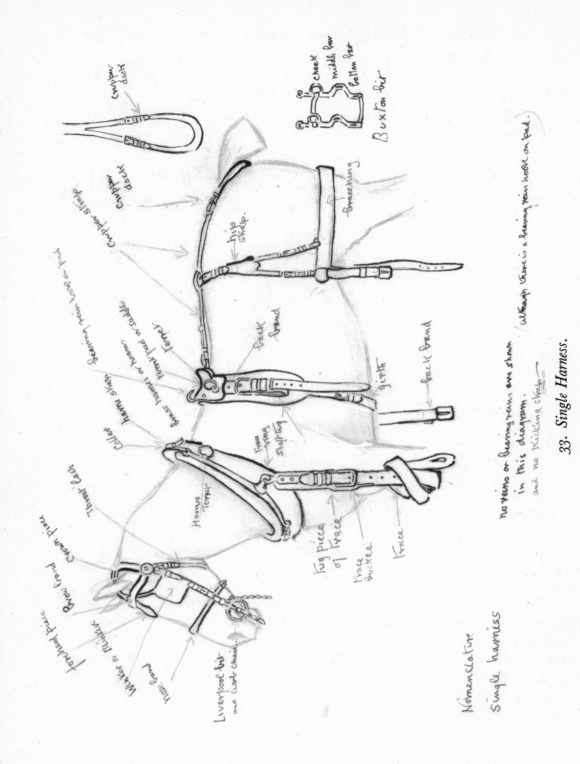

cheek
middle bar
bottom bar

Buxton Bit

crupper dock

crupper dock

Crupper Strap

hip strap.

Breeching

back band

back band

girth

back band

false traces or roomers

loaded pad or saddle

bearing rein hook or pad

terrets

Trace rein shaping

Hames Tommu

Collar

back bearing rein hook or pad

hames shape

Fug Piece of Trace

Trace Buckle

Trace.

Thread Lash

Liverpool bit and Curt Chain

Crown piece

Brow band

Winker or blinker

Nose band

Forehead piece

Nomenclature
Single harness

no reins or bearing reins are shown
in this diagram.
(Although there is a bearing rein hook on pad.
and no kicking strap.

33. *Single Harness.*

own home, and were then sent to Walsall to be burnished. But steel horse furniture requires too much elbow grease and silver sand, especially for those without a groom, so furniture of eglantine has taken its place—nickel is not trustworthy. I have seen a man dragged because his nickel stirrup iron was bent and he was unable to free his foot when merely dismounting from a restive horse.

The fine stitching on harness has always filled me with wonder and admiration. Even today little of it is done by machinery. Women do a certain amount of it as piecework (Walsall again). Modern country saddlers' men can do eight or nine stitches to the inch, while the old harness-makers, working under far from ideal conditions by the light of candles, did as many as twelve fine stitches to the inch. When one takes into consideration the time and material put into its construction, I repeat that it seems strange, especially in view of its cost, how carelessly people treat their harness. Perhaps, therefore, a few tips on harness preservation may not be out of place. Any groom knows them, and many more, but the amateur owner and groom can never compete with the professional. The amateur has too many other things to think of, apart from lack of time.

All harness should be taken to pieces for cleaning. To keep harness pliable it must be kept soft with some form of oil. Colza or linseed should not be used, because they are harmful to leather and become hard (I believe by absorbing oxygen—hence their use by artists). Saddle soap is best for saddles and bridles, because it does not darken the leather or become sticky. For leather which has to be stored for any length of time a petroleum jelly is best. Black leather harness, after the dirt has been removed with a sponge, should be thinly coated with harness compo, and then polished with a soft brush. Patent leather harness merely requires a paraffin rag over it and then a polishing with a dry rubber.

Steel bits and irons (unsuitable for 'without a groom') must be cleaned with silver sand and elbow grease, but alloys should not be touched with anything gritty, such as sand ; they should be washed first, then polished. Brass can best be cleaned with metal polish, of which there are many popular brands on the market. To sum it all up, there are three important things which those without a groom should never forget—the condition of the horse's feet and bowels, and the greasing of the axles of the carriage.

CHAPTER TEN

Highwaymen

MANY hundreds of highwaymen have earned immortality of a sort in the Newgate Calendar ; yet the gentlemen of the road are today a subject of romance. In early days travellers had to move in companies for protection, and of those early days Robin Hood is the legendary robber hero. The greatest period of highway robbery was after the Civil War, when disbanded Royalist and Roundhead soldiers took to the road for a living. Probably most of them still had their arms and horses and had already little to learn about plundering civilians. The first coaches, slow and ponderous, lurching and swaying over the frightful roads of the period, were an easy prey for mounted men. Those roads leading into London were their favourite haunts. In fact, until recent times (comparatively speaking), a troop of horse patrolled the Knightsbridge and Hyde Park area. It is recorded that a trooper (Harris) of the Horse Guards (Blues) in 1704 acted as a highwayman himself and held up a Major Wade at Hounslow. This highwayman was caught and sentenced to death, but got away with it somehow, as the sentence was never carried out.

The eighteenth century would appear to have been the most lucrative period from the highwayman's point of view. The *Bath Chronicle* records quite a number of hold-ups. In the issue of May 26, 1760, appeared the following note :*

On Tuesday last between 9 and 10 o'clock Capt. Grove and Capt. Gossing were returning from Devizes in a post-chaise. They were attacked on Kingsdown by two footpads, one of whom seized the horse of the driver and presented a pistol at his breast, saying at the same time, ' Gentlemen I am prepared for you,' whereupon Capt. Grove jumped out and presented his pistol at the fellow, which he would have discharged, but was afraid of hitting the driver. However, as soon as the footpad released

*From Capt. Spicer's scrapbook, *Recollections of Palmer and the Bath Coaches.*

72

his bridle Capt. Grove fired and he dropped down immediately, dead, but on the Captain going up to him he recovered himself and ran off, as did his companion.

In the issue of March 12, 1763, appeared :

A single highwayman attempted to stop the Exeter Machine near Salisbury. A gentleman having with him five guineas refused to deliver it up and getting out of the coach drew his sword, and gave him challenge, which the cowardly villain refused. The rest of the passengers whereupon took heart and getting round him pulled him from his horse and carried him before a justice, and he was committed to Ilchester Jail.

In the same newspaper on June 16, 1763 :

A few mornings ago the Bath and Bristol Machine was stopped by a single highwayman, who took from the passengers what money they had about them, except one gentleman who concealed his in the skirts of his coat.

In 1769, there was a highwayman who claimed to have ' the best horse in all England '. Unfortunately for him it was by no means ' the willing horse ' for when being chased he was overtaken because the animal refused a small fence ! The horse was shot under him, and ' Mr ' Bracy also mortally wounded. Notice the ' Mr '. Presumably he was of some education, possibly a real gentleman of the road.

A favourite country of highwayman was of course Salisbury Plain, in those days quite unenclosed and providing the ideal get away. Highway robbery was in consequence freely indulged in. Not far from Tilshead on the West Lavington road there is a stone on which is inscribed :

At this spot the Bishop of Wells was attacked and robbed by 4 highwaymen on the evening of October 31, 1839. After a pursuit of 3 hours one, Benjamin Colcough, fell dead on Chiltern Down (presumably from exhaustion). Thomas Saunders, George Waters and Richard Harris were eventually captured, and convicted at the ensuing quarter Sessions at Devizes and transported for a term of 15 years. This monument erected by public subscription as a warning to those who presumptuously think to escape the punishment God has threatened against thieves and robbers.

This must be one of the latest records of that type of highway robbery.

Wiltshire seems to have rather specialized in highway robbery. A

34. Highwayman of the time of Charles II.

notorious rogue, one Thomas Boulter was born at Poulshot near Devizes in 1748.

He began his career as a highwayman from Southampton, where he hired a horse from the Vine Inn. He is next heard of back at Poulshot in 1775 when, in collusion with a maid servant at Erlestoke Manor, he stole a well-known horse, Black Bess, (not Turpin's—Turpin was hanged before this date) from the owner Mr Peter Delme.

Boulter was famous for the great distances he travelled on horseback. He was finally captured near Ripon, Yorkshire, when attempting a hold-up, and was sentenced to death. He was reprieved on the condition he joined the army. He did, and deserted the following week. Boulter then joined up with one James Caldwell and they worked the roads together. However, while they were committing a robbery on the Cheltenham-Gloucester road, the victims retaliated and Boulter was wounded in the eye. This made him easily recognizable and he was again captured, in Dorset. He and Caldwell were both hanged at Winchester in 1778.

In Georgian England there were few highwaymen compared with the number in Stuart and Cromwellian days, and fewer still reached eminence. Nevertheless Sir W. Wynne, when conveying rents from his Welsh estate to bank them in London, took no chances. Harper in *The Holyhead Road* tells us that he had four guards, two on the box and two in the basket of his coach, and one inside with him. Two large dogs ran behind. It was a four or five days journey and at night the two dogs and two of the guards stood sentry over the coach.

Dick Turpin was but a footpad and horse-stealer, but one Jack Rann was the most eminent of the Georgian contemporary gentlemen of the road. He was known as ' 16 String Jack ' from the coloured strings on his knee breeches. His vanity was immense. He appeared at Bagnidge Wells in scarlet and announced himself as the highwayman, ' 16 String Jack '. The company turned him out. His last exploit was the robbing of Princess Amelia's private chaplain. He was shortly after captured. At his trial he wore a suit of pea-green, and died as did most highwaymen, with unmoved bravery. An even more picturesque personage of the time was Captain Maclean. Known as ' the gentleman highwayman ' he was, like Claude Duval, beloved by the ladies, and, indeed, in pursuit of ladies of fortune he obtained the entry into some of the most famous houses, yet in due course he too adorned the gallows tree. But—' If travels on the road seem to us dangerous in those earlier days, do not forget in our times far greater numbers meet death on the road from mechanical vehicles than ever did in the most lawless period of English history.'*

Usually highwaymen were well mounted, presumably on stolen horses, but occasionally they hired from job-masters. In 1774 Lord Berkeley, being held up on Hounslow Heath, fired back at his assailant whose body was afterwards identified by the owner of the horse he had hired.

The most romantic rogue was Claude Duval (tempo Charles II). His dance with the lady on Hounslow Heath has been told many times. Nevertheless his end was most unromantic, as he was caught when very

Travel in England, by Thomas Burke. 1942.

drunk in a public house in Chandos Street.

The Dick Turpin of Harrison Ainsworth's story is a myth and he certainly did not ride to York. The real hero of that exploit was one Nevison by name, who did actually ride on many horses—not one animal —to York. The real Turpin was a peculiarly vicious, low-class rogue of whom nothing good can be said. The end of the highwayman was to be hanged and gibbetted in chains (their bodies were covered with pitch so that they were preserved longer) as a warning to other evil-doers. The improvement in the roads, faster coaches, and armed guards (all very light on the trigger) finished highway robbery as a lucrative trade.

I once was taken to see the haunts of a highwayman in Essex. It was a cottage, and upstairs in the backroom was a stable. I forget what the floor was made of, but in the corner a rack and manger still existed, and a sort of French window acted as both window and door. No one would suspect a stable upstairs, although the window did seem a bit curious ; when I saw it there was no doubt about its being also a door, but probably in those days it was better disguised. How they got a horse upstairs and down was a problem until one realized that the bank rose sharply at the back of the house and it only needed a temporary ramp to lead a horse across into the upper storey.

A friend of mine has the pistol of the last highwayman taken to Winchester jail. Apparently this man held up a mounted farmer near Pitt. The latter knocked the pistol out of the robber's hand and marched the prisoner back to the city and handed him over to the authorities.

That one never hears of police in connection with highwaymen is due to the fact that the police force was only in embryo in those days. A river police force was formed as early as 1798 and there were parochial police in London and environs, who were not of much use one would imagine, as Camberwell, for example, dressed up parish paupers as constables. They were chiefly used to ' move on ' beggars. Then came the Bow Street runners, who acted more as detectives than as police. But the Bow Street patrols, foot (1782) and horse (1805), were more efficient, as was, a little later on, the evening police force, which patrolled from dusk to midnight an area of fifteen miles from Charing Cross to protect the public from highwaymen and footpads. So that even down to 1805 it would appear that highway robbery was not unknown, although I think the mounted highwaymen was by then a *rara avis*.

CHAPTER ELEVEN

'Andmaid to an 'Orse

DURING the throes of cavalry mechanization I was painting an officer's charger in a certain barrack square. The novelty of an artist at work drew a throng of idle soldiers round me, glad of anything to break the monotony of peace-time service. The audience gave, more or less audibly, their opinion of the artist's efforts. This led to conversation, and I endeavoured to find out their reactions to mechanization. A large number were in favour of it, because it would, they thought, be an easier job, and there would be less of ' stables, stables, stables ! ' One youth, a recent recruit, said he didn't agree.

' Fancy my swotting up 'ere to enlist, entirely to be with 'osses, and now look wot I'm let in for ! '

' Pah ! ' said another recruit. ' No accounting for tastes. I didn't join the Army to be an 'andmaid to an 'orse.'

Now I wondered at the time if this latter opinion (apparently one frequently held) meant that in post-war days we would be faced with a shortage of grooms. An old stud groom gave as his opinion that, although hunting would go on, ' gents would have to do their own horses'. Now I am inclined to think that up to a point he was right, but what he entirely forgot is the girl groom. There are, I think, no lack of these. Of course, their entry into that sacred sanctuary, the saddle room, was looked on with horror by the elderly, but it was bound to come, and doubtless they are quite as efficient as the average male, and their light weight and gentler methods may be an improvement on many of the old ' kim over ! ' school.

The saddle-room was the sanctum, or rather throne room of the Victorian coachman, an autocratic being whose word was law, and the brightly polished harness and other horse furniture were his crown jewels which gaily reflected the saddle-room fire. It seemed, on wintry days, to be the last word in comfort to a small boy who was allowed by that august personage to poke about the stables, climb into the loft, and

35. *Carriage and pair, 1900.*

fall into the corn bin and generally make himself a nuisance. Doubtless small boys (even the master's sons) were pretty bad, but what *would* he have said to girl grooms ?

The old type of coachman was an aristocrat who knew his job and saw that his underlings were taught theirs. An elderly groom, now in the motor trade, told me that, when he was a lad, he started in private stables, his job being tack cleaning.

One day the coachman set him to clean a set of pair horse harness. When finished, he hung it up. The head coachman said, ' Take it down and clean it again '. He did so, taking it all to pieces and polishing every buckle, and then hung it up again.

' Take it down and do it again ! ' said the coachman.

' What have I done wrong ? ' said the lad.

' You hung it up with the head pieces the wrong way round. Have you never noticed that the near horse has a rosette on the left side and the off side horse's rosette is on the right ? Now hang them up properly, so that when taken down each is put on the correct horse.'

The groom told me, ' I never forgot that lesson. It has even been useful in the garage, for it taught me observation and tidiness.'

Those of us who remember income tax at a shilling in the pound also remember how much less strenuous were those days. We did not live in a hurry, partly because we could not do otherwise. The pace of the horse regulated our lives, and consequently the stables were (next the kitchen) the most important part of most establishments, especially in the country ; although even in London it was the horsed bus and the hansom cab which regulated our daily timetable.

I miss, in these mechanical days, the friendly atmosphere of the old stables, more particularly the Sunday morning visit to the stables after church. It literally was a church parade. The head man met you at the stable door with a sieve containing sliced carrots or apples, to give to the horses, which were examined in turn and their praises sung for the benefit of the visitor. The stables were especially smart, pillar reins whitened, all buckles polished, the partitions and the straw bed both finished off with plaited straw, and at the stable doors your crest or initials were gorgeously displayed on the floor in coloured sands. Somehow all this is entirely lacking in the garage. The slightly supercilious chauffeur of today is sadly deficient in *joie de vivre*, and it certainly isn't that, by comparison, he is overworked ! The coachman and stablemen worked far longer hours—indeed, they had no fixed period of working hours. How often have I seen a red-nosed, muffled-up coachman in London or the suburbs, walking his horses slowly up and down for hours on end, long after street and carriage lamps were lit, waiting for an unpunctual and inconsiderate master or mistress.

Yet there was then, nevertheless, a kindlier feeling between master and man. I recall one inconsiderate business man who kept his coach-man up to all hours. One night he dismissed his carriage near the stables and started to walk home. The coachman handed the reins to his groom and hurried away. Presently he came back out of breath and distressed. ' Good gracious, Mr West, where have 'ee been ? ' said the groom. ' To take a last look at master,' he replied. ' I shan't see him no more.' A strange premonition of death, for he died the following day. (West was born and died in the service of the same family.)

I think on the whole a coachman had a good life. He was housed, clothed (livery and stable suits) free, and usually both coal and light were included. In the country most masters also gave vegetables and milk. His wage would be from thirty-five shillings to two pounds a week (and the pound was worth twenty shillings in those days). The groom under him would earn eighteen shillings (twenty-five shillings in London and board out), lodging, coal and light, while ' perks ' were considerable. Stable commission (although not a fixed rate) usually brought a coachman in five per cent on all forage, saddlery and clothing, one shilling per set from the blacksmith's account, five per cent on vets' bills and so on, not to mention tips from his master's visitors. This commission system was firmly established and, if not approved of, was at least overlooked by many horse-owners, although a few fought it strenu-ously.

With city men who were too busy to attend to anything but their own affairs, and who were in any case ignorant of stable management, no doubt the coachmen ' feathered his nest ', being no better, or worse, than other people. I remember one coachman, Roberts by name, who saved enough to start as a small livery-stable keeper. He ran a couple of cabs to and from the station for many years until his death.

Unfortunately they were not always sufficiently far-sighted to live on their wages with sensible economy and thus make a modest provision for old age. For I knew another Roberts, who sank from head coachmen with men under him to be the doctor's coachman—a real hard job of day and night work. From this he descended to hotel ostler, and, out-living the days of the horse, he ended up as ' boots ' in a small commercial hotel in a provincial town.

When the coachman's master had ' company ', the visitors' carriage horses, with rugs across their loins, stood in the long row of stalls on the pillar reins (pillar chains in some cases), while the drivers adjourned to the harness room to play cards. The game was, I think, always nap. Stalls have vanished out of modern stables, for, with far fewer horses, the necessity for saving room is gone, and we think today that the animals do better in boxes, which I feel sure is correct. Stalls, all the same, were an economy not only of space but of labour. With regard to the latter, far less straw is wasted, and there is less ' mucking out ' to do. Today this may seem strange. In my district straw is almost *embarras de richesse*, or was until recently. As a result of the great increase in arable farming there was an abundance, so that it was even burnt at times. Yet such is the congestion and cost of rail traffic that in some counties it was difficult to obtain.

In London of the 'nineties I remember well the importance of the straw question. As a student I lived in a Kensington back room overlook-ing a mews. In the morning the first sound I heard was the clatter of horses' hooves and the swish of water as carriages were washed down, while in summer time a strong smell of horse urine ascended and entered my open window. Not that I ever objected to it, for, my foster mother having been the wife and also the daughter of a coachman, I was presum-ably early accustomed to the aroma. I remember that in the dog days of the season the London streets all smelt of hot tar and horse quite as strongly as they do of petrol in similar weather today. A country squire of my acquaintance was quite unable to face London in the season (much to the annoyance of his wife), as the former smell gave him horse asthma. With the coming of the mechanical age this disability has entirely dis-appeared, he tells me.

To return to the mews. Most London stables consisted of two stalls and a coach-house with a flat overhead. The stalls were narrow and there was little room to avoid any animal that was ' a bit light behind '. There were two doors, one which led into the cobble-stoned

F

36. Sunday morning after church in Victorian days.

mews and the other to the stairs which led up to the coachmen's quarters, for he and his family lived above his charges. I expect modern sanitary inspectors would condemn this system, but it certainly was not noticeable that the usually large families of coachmen were any less healthy than those of other and better-housed mortals. Stuffy his quarters were, and more especially so his stables, where a naked gas jet flared all day long; the heat largely accounted for the lovely satin-like coats of the carriage horses, and, combined with unnecessarily tight bearing reins, was why they so frequently went wrong in the wind. The fact that in London straw was expensive was largely responsible for the aforementioned smell, as it was turned and dried and used again, with complete disregard to Hayes, who says with reference to straw : ' It is owing to its feeble power of absorption, etc., that to preserve straw bedding in a sweet smelling-state we are obliged to reject a large portion of it at each " mucking-out ".'

To return to the country : just as the modern stud-groom comes in each evening to get his orders and report on lame or convalescent animals, so the coachman used to receive his instructions on the previous day, such as ' Saddle horse at 10 a.m., Pair for garden-party at 3.0 p.m., Dog-cart for committee meeting,'—and so on. But emergency orders were very far from popular. ' Carriage at once for the station ! ' might catch the coachman unshaved, with his top boots and breeches of the previous day neither dry nor cleaned. A friend of mine told me : ' Our particular man's shaving always intrigued me as a boy. He would take a leather girth and give his razor two or three strops on it. Dipping the razor into one of the several buckets of cold water that were always left standing about, and making various suitable contortions, he would draw it up and down, and in two minutes it was done. But to hear the razor scraping off that stiff stubble was a sound I've never forgotten. Moreover this man swore he never used soap for shaving, and that he had only had two razors in his life ! '

Perhaps the weakest spot of the profession was that there was nothing to prevent any man calling himself a groom or coachman, no matter how ignorant of horses he might be. Yet the intelligent execution of their job is certainly not within the compass of everyone, by any means. Consequently ' a good character ' given with a man was all you had as a guide to go on, and, since many employers were singularly slack about the accuracy of their statements (as I know to my cost), you occasionally got wrong 'uns—the worst being the bad-tempered variety who vented their rage on their horses on the slightest provocation. However, you usually soon found them out, for quiet horses became nervous or ' nappy ', or even developed bunged-up eyes. (You were told ' They 'ave 'it theirself '.) None-the-less, in spite of exceptions, as a race English grooms and coachmen were easily the best in Europe, and it was an unwritten law, scrupulously observed, that, in the event of the horse or horses getting out of hand and bolting, the coachman, like the captain at sea, was always the last man to abandon ship.

However, with the passing of the horse the coachman has also departed, and in these days a stud-groom reigns in his stead over a sadly diminished establishment, a real stud-groom being found, as a rule, only in stables of over a dozen horses. Today the majority are working stud-grooms, usually quite as efficient, if not quite so immaculate in the cut of their breeches and gaiters.

Coming to the single-handed grooms most of us employed, I recall a story of a North Country groom who was called in to assist the parlour-maid at a small country dinner party. Being told by the maid to hand the potatoes he arrived at the guest's side and took off the dish-cover, then whisked the dish away again saying : ' Aw, dommit, 'tis cabbage ! '

Last, but not least in the list, comes the groom-gardener, who by most employers is expected to do the impossible, and, strange to relate, sometimes does ! Such a one, whom we will call George, successfully looked after his master's gundogs, his mistress's one hunter, the children's rabbits, two hound puppies, a goat, and the stable cat. One evening after George had gone home his mistress brought back a brood of young ducks, and left a note for George to feed them first thing in the morning. Next day master, shaving at an open window, heard George say to the housemaid as he fed the ducks : ' Well, I reckon that now all we require in this place is a dromedary and then we'd 'ave our own Whipsnade ! '

However, let us return to London and the naughty 'nineties. As it is amusing and not unprofitable to notice changes and trace improvements (in some things, but by no means everything) let me recall the period as I remember it. London, at any rate outwardly, was more splendid, and certainly more impressive as our capital city, than it is today.

Recently, on one of the rare occasions on which I go to town, I walked through a familiar Kensington square. It was a bright summer's day, but gloom encircled me as I passed notices which read ' Board Residence ', ' Private Hotel ', ' Apartments '. The street was empty save for a taxi on the old cab rank at the end of the square. I recall passing through that square forty years ago, also on a bright summer's day. Every house had a window box, gay with flowers. Most houses had bright-coloured sun blinds, and a smart carriage and pair waited outside more than one door—sleek bay horses, shining harness, and smart servants in new liveries. At the end of the square stood two hansom cabs, with good-looking old screws in the shafts. Both were turned out remarkably smartly, at any rate compared with the old growler (four-wheeler) which shared the cab rank. Outside another house two hacks were being led up and down ; judging by the groom's stable dress they were hirelings, for only a few people bought their own hacks, as well as their carriage horses, up to London for the season. In addition a butcher's cart, with a smart cob in the shafts, rattled by delivering a belated order. The London butchers were famous for their smart cobs and turn-outs. The drivers in their blue aprons and smooth plastered-down hair, sitting high above their box-like vehicles, were great artists in driving at top speed through thick traffic. Yet I never remember one in collision. It was the private Jehu who most often got into trouble—perhaps because ' John' was brought up from the country when the family came to town for the season, and the traffic was very different from that on country roads.

This style of coachman usually drove with a rein in each hand, and much too long a rein at that, so that his hands were near his own nose. The result was that if the vehicle in front pulled up suddenly, he nearly fell over backwards in stopping his own animal or animals. Frequently the pole of his carriage went through the back of the one in front.

I always remember a story of an elderly aunt, whose victoria, although in no way involved in an accident of this kind, was delayed for some little time while the victims disentangled themselves. Tired of waiting, she suddenly announced to her lady companion : ' I'm going to scream !' —and scream she did. Up rushed a police inspector. ' It's all right, milady, you're in no danger ! Constable let this lady through !' The aunt gave him a sweet smile and her carriage and her conversation continued as before.

At that time London was full of handsome vehicles. Hyde Park and St James's Park were thronged in the season with sight-seers, especially on Drawing Room or Levee days, and the sight was worth seeing. As a matter of detail, and a typical sign of the times, heraldic painters of those days were kept busy indicating pictorially, by signs and emblems, the ownership of these highly varnished vehicles.

Today most of these elegant equipages have long vanished into dust, but changes of taste and fashion took place long before the motor age, and we are told that about the time of the accession of Queen Victoria, ' the hackney cabs which plied for hire in London were often the cast-off family coaches of the nobility, despoiled of their gorgeous hammer cloths that seated the coachmen in front and the carved stand that supported one or two footmen behind in their former halycon days '

A few of these private state coaches are still in being, standing hidden away and shrouded in dust sheets in the coach-houses of the great ; but they now seldom, if ever, see the light of day, for the lack of suitable carriage horses (even for hire) has precluded their use at such functions as jubilees and coronations in recent years.

Remarkably few artists painted pictures of the elegant equipages of the late Victorian period. It was the last age of pageantry, and it seems to me they missed a great opportunity (as we so often do if it is right beneath our noses), although the coaching age had artists who made that subject peculiarly their own, such as Pollard, Cooper Henderson and Herring. Yet few vehicles other than coaches have been immortalized. At any rate pictures of private vehicles are scarce, although very occasionally one comes across portraits of people painted sitting in their carriages, such as that of Mr Stanley Massey driving his cabriolet, by John Ferneley, 1830, which I saw in the Tate Gallery, probably on loan, as remarkably few sporting pictures can be seen in our public galleries.

Perhaps the courtyard of Burlington House on the day of the Academy private view was the show-piece of the London season, and no picture on the walls could compete with that seen outside. The crowd of servants with top hats, stand up collars, white gloves, and dark coloured liveries of the comparatively impecunious, and the cocked hats, gold lace, plush breeches, silk stockings and buckled shoes of the Royal households, or of the merely rich, were in themselves a spectacle. The tossing heads, and silver and gold plated harness of the horses, and the marvellous varnished carriages made a picture which astonishing to relate was never painted by contemporary artists.

I recall with distinct nostalgia many sights and sounds that have departed from London—even such trivial things as the almost uncanny silence when iron-tyred vehicles were driven over the fifty yards of straw laid down in the road in front of a house where a sick man lay. When did rubber tyres come in, do you say ? I think about 1897 or 1898.

I miss the Dalmation dog running not beside, but under my lady's victoria ; the bright ribbons and rosettes in her horses' brow-bands ; and the tiny ' Tiger ' standing in front of the phaeton pair, or sitting with folded arms when she drove herself.

37. ' When the coachman's master had "company", the visitors' carriage horses, with rugs across their loins, stood in the long rows of stalls on the pillar reins . . .'

CHAPTER TWELVE

Tourist Coaching in the Nineties

COACH tours were as popular in the 'nineties as they are today, but they were then horsed coaches. These were gradually superseded by the motor coach, which was able to carry more passengers over greater distances in less time.

The centres of tourist traffic were then, as now, North Wales, the Scottish Highlands, the West Country and the Lake District.

My own experience is confined to Wales and Devon. For many forgotten details of Welsh coaching I am indebted to J. Francis of Colwyn Bay, who often drove the *Venture* for his father, who ran a number of coaches from that centre. The Llandudno Coaching Company also put a number of coaches on the road every season : among others, a daily coach from Caernavon through Llanberis. One Colwyn Bay coach the *Duke of York* did a grand, long tour daily of fifty-six miles. Leaving at 10 a.m. it went up the Vale of Conway to the Waterloo Hotel, Bettws-y-Coed (lunch 12.15, changed horses, left at 1.15 sharp) on to Capel Curig, keeping to the Holyhead road to Ogwen Lake, Bethesda, Llandegai, Aber, Llanfairfechan ; a change of horses again, and (just time for tea) home via Penmaenmawr and Conway to Colwyn Bay at 6.30 p.m. The fare was ten shillings.

This coach was speeded up, and for the last stage an extra good team was harnessed which could do the last thirteen miles in very good time, as previously passengers had often complained they had not time to change for dinner. Another coach, *The Old Times*, left Colwyn Bay 11 a.m. for Llandullas, Abergele, where the coach pulled up at the Bee Hotel, which until fairly recent times had immense stabling accommodation, and gave one some idea of road traffic in the real coaching era, as did The Plough Inn at St. Asaph—also once a famous coaching house— at which the passengers lunched, returning to Colwyn Bay via the Marble Church.

Another coach, the *Venture*, left at 11 a.m. for Abergele, Llanfairtalhairn and Llangerniew, where passengers lunched at the Stag Hotel and walked up through Hafordinas Hall, viewing the gardens, to meet the coach on the upper road. The way back was via the Holland Arms (for tea), a very old inn with the sign ' This gate hangs well '. I forget the rest of the inscription, but remember that a haunch of venison always hung on the gate. This coach returned to Colwyn Bay at 6.15 p.m. Fare six shillings for thirty-five miles.

The coach I personally remember best was the *Sportsman*, which I often met as it came over Conway Suspension Bridge, with the guard blowing his horn to announce their approach to the toll keeper (the toll was two shillings each way). This coach was driven by Willie Wotherspoon, a very exceptional driver, who died only recently. The coach left at 2.30 and returned at 6 p.m., having driven through Conway and Sychnant Pass, and returned via Penmaenmawr and Conway. At the Echo Stone, half way down the Pass, the horn was always blown. The echo was very popular with the ' Tow Rows ' as the Welsh rudely call our tourists. The only accident of any note in Welsh coaching took place in this Pass to a Llandudno coach (I think the *Tally Ho*). Going down, the brakes broke, just past the Echo, and the coach ran into the low wall on the right. The driver and several passengers tumbled off and rolled down the steep side. Although bruised and shaken no one was seriously injured. The horses, which naturally bolted, were stopped in Dwygyfylchi village at the bottom. All these coaches were the real thing and not charabancs. The *Old Times, Venture* and *Sportsman* were the old original type of stage coach with inside seating for from four to six people, originally built to carry fourteen persons. They were converted by sinking wells in the roof and extending the seats each side to hold an extra passenger. They then carried four fives and two on the box seat, making twenty-two passengers.

The other coaches were of more recent date and were ' dummies '. They all had a boot in which was carried spare traces, shoeing tools, front and hind shoes, etc., as most coachmen could tack on a shoe in those days. The coachmen (carrying on tradition) were great dandies even in these public conveyances and very fussy over their dress, in wet weather wearing a thick melton coat, with a cape with pleats in it, like the old stage coachmen. They wore very low beaver hats, and usually only one glove (the left). In summer both driver and guard wore white

38. Tourist coaching in North Wales in the 'nineties.

coats and white top hats. The driver's coat was double-breasted.

Most of these old coachmen have now passed away, but Will Roberts and Will Mawr (an enormous man), Jim Murphy and Rowdy Downes are names I recall, and of Llandudno drivers, Oliver Clark, Fred Fox and Jack Emlin.

These coaches were well horsed and needed to be. I can see those horses now with the sweat pouring off them as they pulled a heavy load of humanity up Welsh hills, or rattled down with screaming brakes amid clouds of dust. (This was before the days of tar macadam.) The horses were usually of hunter type, and almost never of hackney blood. They were remarkably fit at the end of the coaching season, and the sound ones were in demand for hunters. The remainder were usually turned out to rough it for the winter and, more often than not, were sound again by next coaching season.

Some of my earliest recollections are of tourist coaches in North Devon, where I often went for the school holidays. There were the coaches running between Minehead and Lynton, and one, the *Red Deer*, remains in my memory as the only coach I actually saw using a ' cockhorse '. The word ' cockhorse ' probably conveys nothing to modern readers, but if described as a trace horse, the term is explained to urban readers, who probably have often seen one in use in London, for there are, or were until quite recently, such trace horses belonging to one or other of the animal protection societies to be seen almost daily helping heavily laden animals up the slippery inclines of Tower Hill, Knightsbridge, Highgate, and similar places. Cockhorses had ordinary collars, but these collars had no rings or terrets. Long saddle flaps on the ridden horse covered the stirrup leathers, only the irons being visible. They had ordinary carriage headstalls and bits, but riding reins. There was a loin strap to hold up the trace, and two others from the crupper strap to hold up the swingle bar, apparently to keep it from too much lateral motion, and also possibly to keep it away from the tail. Two cockhorses, one ridden postilion fashion, were sometimes used on bad hills. There was always one on Porlock Hill, which has (although the road has been improved) so often been the undoing of motor drivers of late years. I do not know if the law ever took any action against coaches being overloaded, but, human nature being what it is, tourists, I know, frequently objected to getting down and walking up steep hills, saying they had paid their fares to be carried. Nevertheless, I am glad to say they were usually made to walk by a strong-minded driver and guard.

The Minehead coach, the *Red Deer*, started from the Plume of Feathers opposite the railway station. At the Ship Inn, Porlock, the passengers dismounted and proceeded to climb 1,000 feet in one and a half miles. I believe the gradient is one in four, so no wonder it required an extra horse ! As far as I can remember the passengers remounted after the worst and first part of the hill was climbed and the combined teams pulled them up to the crest on Porlock Common. At Culbone stables horses were changed (they really were stables until quite recently). I cannot remember if there was a toll at County Gate farther along, but it certainly looks as if it had been a ' pike ' at some time. I always thought coming down Porlock Hill even more alarming than coming down the Countisbury one. I wrote to the Rev. H. J. Marshall on the subject, and he replied : Two coaches used to run, the *Lorna Doone* which belonged to Baker of the Castle Hotel, Lynton. It was driven

39. *View from the box seat of a 1914 coach showing the arrangement of the coach harness.* **Below left:** *on old coaches, the leader's reins were passed through a ring between the wheeler's ears ;* **right:** *on more modern vehicles, the rein passed through a ring at the side.*

by Tom Baker, a first-class whip—I saw him drive between the *Red Deer* standing outside the Castle Inn, Porlock, and the cottage railings opposite, at full trot, the wheels only just clearing. The *Red Deer* ran the reverse route from Minehead to Lynton. The two coaches usually met in Porlock ; with red coats and horns blowing and full of passengers, they made a fine sight . . . '

Coming down Porlock Hill was, as I said before, a fearsome business, and it took some driving, as the vehicles were apt to skid. I remember the surface was kept rough to give a foothold for the horses, and also to hold the slipper, which cut deep groves in the road. None-the-less, a former driver of these coaches, after having his first journey by train to Taunton, said he felt ' a lot safer on the box of the coach '. The *Lorna Doone* ran until about 1920 when it was superseded by a motor. Curtis, the last

40. ' *Jockey Carriage* ', *Scarborough, 1880-90.*

driver of this coach is still alive, I believe. It used to be said that Rook, who kept the Ship Inn at the foot of Porlock Hill, derived much profit from restoring the shattered nerves of passengers who had just descended the hill ! Countisbury was nearly as alarming owing to the presence of the sea so near at hand, although 100 feet below. Nevertheless the coach descended at a full trot. Once an unfortunate rider took the sea side when meeting the coach in a narrow place. His horse shied and they both went over the parapet and down the cliff. The rider escaped by a miracle. Mr Marshall remarked, ' rule of the road, or no, I always took the inside when riding up Countisbury Hill '.

The *Lorna Doone* ended by doing short afternoon trips to the Doone Valley (Malmsmead)—a sad come-down from its palmy days. Eventually it was done away with altogether.

I might add that Scarborough had a form of tourist traffic peculiar to itself. I remember seeing what they locally called jockey carriages, which plied for hire in that town. My illustration shows one of these.

CHAPTER THIRTEEN

Just Horses

IN those far off days when the yeomanry were yeomen, that force was remarkable in more ways than one. Originally formed for home defence at the time of Napoleon's theatened invasion of this country, they retained, almost up to the time of mechanization, as their full dress, (at any rate in Hussar units) a gorgeous uniform full of buttons and braid, little changed from the Napoleonic age, making the mere regular look like a plucked pullet in comparison. In the early days other ranks were almost entirely composed of farmers, and in those times when farming was farming, these troopers brought their own horses to the summer training camps. I remember an old farrier sergeant of the North Devon Yeomanry telling me that, when he first joined as a youth, some of the hill farmers brought in mares that had only recently foaled, so that when they paraded for squadron drill, the first order before mounting was ' Milk your mares '. This old boy died some thirty years ago in his seventy-ninth year, so that it is going back quite a bit. I remember telling this tale to his squadron commander, the late Lord Fortescue, who said : ' I remember him quite well. He was a terrible old boy to talk ; but I believe his story to be quite true.'

As times changed so did the type of yeoman, and with the exception of some few units, the farmers were replaced by recruits from the towns, and so horses had to be found for them. These were usually supplied by contractors, who horsed the mounted units for their summer training the same horses in many cases going on from one training camp to another so that while the first unit might get horses strange to the work, the last one to receive them got horses, who, although they might look a bit the worse for wear, at least knew their job. A little later when mechanization was in the wind, it was rightly argued that one of the great difficulties the territorial artillery in particular had to face was that so few recruits had any previous experience of horses, so their short period of training was wasted trying to make horsemen of them, instead of training them

41. *Officer and trooper in full dress
uniform of a regiment of
Yeomanry Hussars.*

to shoot. So, to the territorial army, at that time the much-debated
mechanization was a blessing in disguise, although half the fun of camp
life departed with the horse.

Some of these contractors' horses were strange animals. A certain
hired troop horse became famous at Military Sports as a show jumper
winning many prizes for its regiment. After the summer training this
animal was sent to Cave's Repository in Birmingham for sale. It was
bought by the territorial trooper who had ridden it in camp. He entered

it at the local Horse Show, but after knocking down several fences, the horse bolted through the crowd with him. Very much annoyed, he took the animal home and fairly put it through it, with the result it bolted again. He turned it out and the following spring he sold it at auction, and it was bought by the same firm of contractors, who later issued it to the same unit, and so it fell to our ' terrier ' to ride it again. He did so with some misgiving, but at the regimental sports the horse displayed its previous brilliant form at jumping with him on its back in uniform. It was then entered for a brigade sports event, when as the competition was likely to be pretty hot, it was thought advisable to school the animal over stiffer obstacles. Taking off his uniform, for it was hot, the trooper went down to the schooling ground in shirt sleeves and trousers. The animal refused and then bolted. Explanation, please ! My only suggestion is that the animal was originally schooled by a civilian who knocked it about, but that it had always been well treated by horse-loving soldiers.

At a contractor's stables, two vanners (geldings) not only worked together in double harness, but slept in adjoining stalls. As is (or was) usual in commercial stables, the partitions were only slung bales. At night one of the animals slipped its head collar, and, getting into the adjoining stall, worried its partner with its teeth, so that the animal was so severely damaged as to be laid up for months. I can cap this story from my own experience. My thoroughbred gelding and a hackney mare stood in adjoining boxes for years, yet one day, when the gelding was turned out with the hackney and a pony mare, he attacked the former. As she was unable to outdistance the thoroughbred, she was eventually cornered. The gelding then got her down and was using his teeth when I arrived on the scene with a stick. It is even stranger, I think, that a gelding should attack a mare, than that stable companions should fall out.

I have heard many arguments on equine intelligence or the lack of it. It is very easy to take the latter view, since one is bound to confess to having seen horses do more foolish things than sensible ones. Although their intelligence may be limited and their reasoning power small, one cannot but wonder if they have, apart from instinct, another extra sense that we do not possess : the ability to see what is unseen by human eyes— a sort of second sight. You may laugh and welcome, but the fact remains that I once saw both horse and hounds afraid of something that

G

was quite invisible to me, and a friend who lives in the environs of Exmoor, tells me that at a certain cross-roads where five lanes meet (you can easily identify the place on a map) their horses (or more strictly speaking any new horses that they purchase) always shy. As far as is known there is no reason for this, and the fact that possibly there was once a gibbet at these cross-roads can scarcely affect equine nerves today.

There are lots of equine incidents I have come across or been told by reliable witnesses that seem difficult to explain satisfactorily. In a certain contractor's yard were two ' vanners ', a mare and a gelding, who worked together in double harness for several years. Eventually the mare went hopelessly lame, so she was shot in the archway between the two stable yards. The gelding continued to work in single harness after her death, but from that day would not pass through the archway—though he had not seen the mare destroyed.

It is well known that white horses were once worshipped by the peoples of Upper Europe as symbols of purity, and they have always been considered lucky. For example, some thirty years ago I owned a very good-looking white hunter, and was frequently greeted by children with, ' White horse, white horse, give me good luck,' and ' place a six-pence neath my foot '. In the days before riding tours became popular, but after the introduction of motor transport, I took the afore-mentioned horse down to Wales with me. Horses were very seldom seen in mountain-ous districts where there was no hunting. I well remember riding over the hills to Portmadoc via Blaenau Festiniog, and at the latter place being accosted by a small boy, who said, ' Well indeed, when wass the circus coming ?' I trust it was the horse and not its rider that reminded him of the circus.

42. Yeomanry at dismounted sword drill.

CHAPTER FOURTEEN

Farm Vehicles

THE mechanization of our farms is now so rapid that the time is at hand when agricultural horse-drawn vehicles will have vanished as completely as our carriages of fifty years ago. I have therefore included in these pages one or two of the vehicles still in use although in ever-decreasing numbers. Agricultural vehicles have passed through more than one crisis in the past, but they will scarcely survive mechanization. In Hertfordshire in 1622 it was actually proposed that four-wheeled carts should be suppressed, and an edict prohibited any carrier or other person from travelling with any wares-cart or carriage with more than two wheels containing more than twenty cwt. or drawn by more than five horses. By the middle of the eighteenth century many Acts had been passed for the purpose of preserving the very dubious highways. In particular the width of wheels was the subject of many restrictions and wagons were allowed to pay less toll in proportion to the width of their wheels. However, in the end the object of preserving the roads by adapting the traffic to the roads failed, and the roads had at long last to be adapted to the traffic. The Highway Act of 1835 removed all restrictions. Not long ago the carriage of flour, manure, coal and similar goods was done by a carter and his team, but of late years the horse has disappeared on farms except for cultivation and the tractor is hastening his departure even from this sphere. There is, or rather was, a different type of wagon in almost every county. Farm wagons, millers' and brewers' drays are now seldom seen, as apart from mechanization, trollies seem to have taken their place. A return to the simplest form of vehicle, shorn of all picturesque elaboration, hermaphrodite wagons, known as 'mophrodites' are common in Lincolnshire. In these the hind part can be detached and used as a two-wheeled cart.

In Gloucestershire you can still sometimes see a beautiful hoop-raved wagon, almost the oldest form of wagon. Today farm wagons have almost gone—even two-wheeled carts are comparatively seldom

43. Milk Float, 1905.
' *It would slowly jog off home with " maister ", always safely delivering him* '.

*44.   Cart harness of the midland and southern counties of England used in shaft-
vehicles.   (Drawn in Hampshire, 1940.)*

seen—and, curiously enough, milk floats, once in universal use on farms,
are now more often seen delivering milk in our streets ; they have vanished off the farms since motor milk-lorries now visit all but the most remote
places.

The illustration of the milk float recalls an old farmer I knew who
usually drove into market behind a cob called The Curate, his other
passengers being calves, or pigs beneath a pig net. Having disposed of
these he would adjourn to the local hostelry, and when he had attained
a sufficiently deep slumber, his pals would place him in his milk float,
put the pig net over him, tie the reins loosely to the dashboard and smack
the old cob on its backside when it would slowly jog off home with
' maister ', safely delivering him to his fat good natured ' missus ', who

45. *A gambo—a primitive type of cart sketched in Cardiganshire, 1946.*

12 spokes

14 spokes

46. *Sussex wagon still in use at Ringmer in 1947, and said to be 175 years old.*

47. Cob or milk-float harness . . . .

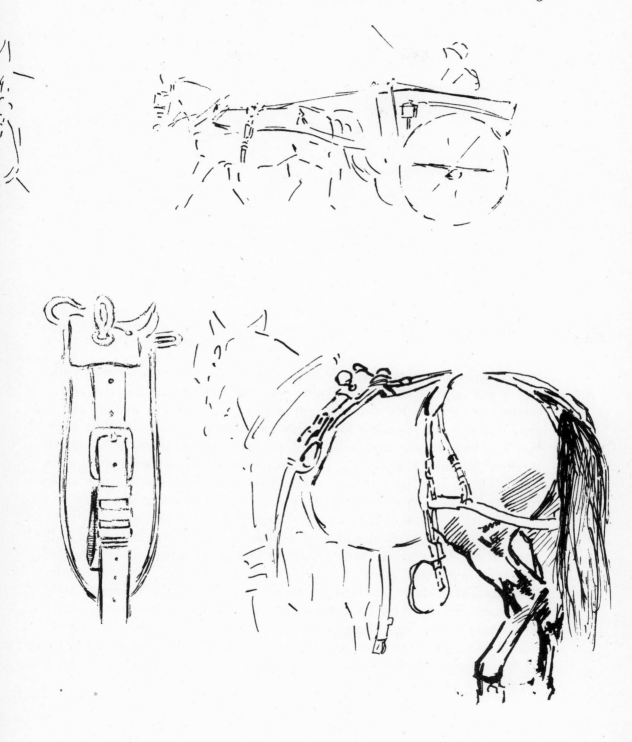

. . . . *Pony harness for tub cart.*

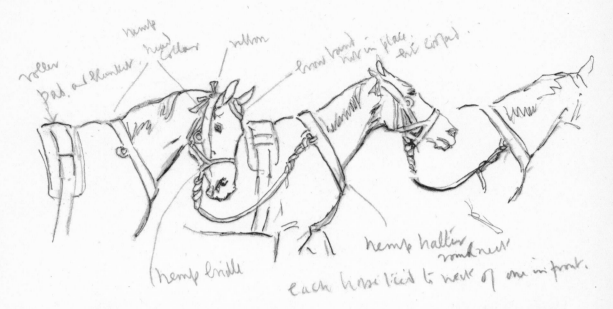

48. Horse-dealers going to fairs led three or four horses each tied not head to tail but to each other's necks—or rather, shoulders.

looked with a comparatively lenient eye on his weekly misdemeanour,

I notice that the horse-dealer (in later times often a gypsy) also seems to have disappeared from our roads. I remember seeing such a one, riding a pony leading four horses head to tail. Actually they were tied by a head rope to another head rope round the shoulders of the horse in front (see my illustration). The animals were usually gaily decorated with ribbons and straw-plaited manes and tails. The last I saw on the road was in West Wales two or three years ago *en route* to a local fair.

There is almost as much variety in farm harness as there is in vehicles. In Southern Scotland and Northern England, the horses (all Clydesdales) wear black harness with steel hames, hexagonal steel buckles and ornaments, and often a ' long ' collar (see Fig. 50). In the South-West and Midlands cart harness is usually decorated with brass fittings, and more often than not collars have wooden hames (the latter frequently with a metal covering). Brass-headed nails are freely used for the decoration of pad and of box housing. The mention of brass decorations bring us to the subject of horse brasses, bells, and the like. Wagon bells were

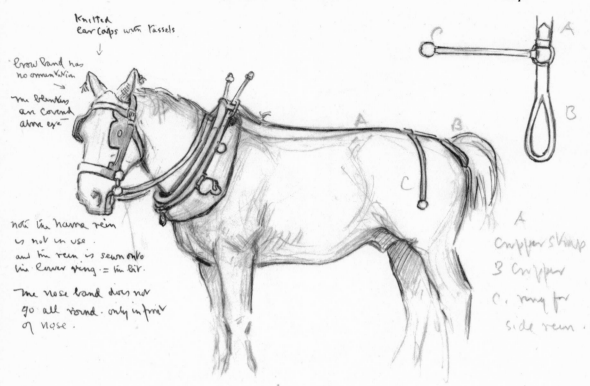

49. Trace, or plough, harness, 1940.

originally used to warn other traffic of the approach of huge wagons. In the early days usually eight-horsed, they latterly had a four-horse team all with bells. The sets were made up of four rings of bells (occasionally more) and were attuned to different notes. These bells had different names in different counties. In Hampshire, latten bells; in Sussex, horse bells; in Hereford, a hoop of bells; in Somerset, a chime (or box) of bells. Latten is the old English name for a mixed metal—an alloy of brass. These bells were fixed in a box housing, often called the frame. According to a Hampshire farmer, the shaped irons or prongs on this frame fitted into sockets or pockets in the horse's collar. A Somerset farmer tells me they were bound with thongs to the wooden hames, but a Sussex farmer says, 'In my set the bells were attached to a frame with spronk holders. These were slipped into square iron staples on the hame woods (commonly called "hamoods")'. The hames were always made

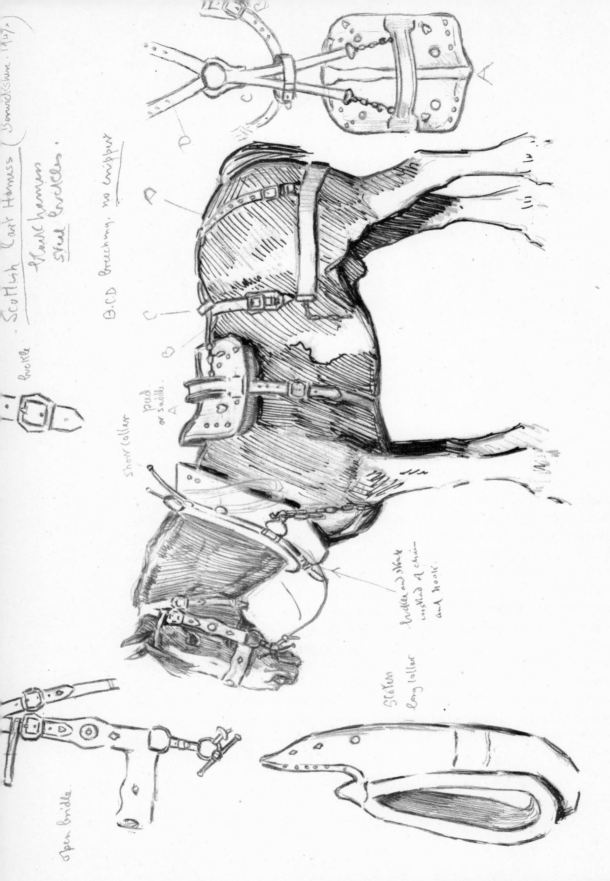

- Scottish Cart Harness (Berwickshire 1947)

Plenn harness
Steel buckles.

B.C.D Breeching, no crupper

Buckle

Short Collar

Pad
or saddle.

Bridle and Hook
washed a chain
and hook

Staken
long collar

Open bridle

50. Scottish cart harness, Berwickshire, 1947.

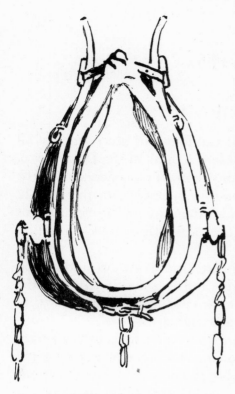

*51. Modern cart collar,
south and west of England.*

of ashwood in Sussex (the tug hooks were also fixed to the 'hamoods'). One never sees these staples on the hames now, except on a very old pair. 'Bell teams' were common enough sixty years ago. As before mentioned there were four sets of bells. The lead horse had five bells, the lash four bells, the body four bells, the wheel or shaft horse three bells. Each set of bells made its own chord and rang two major octaves, the complete set making a most pleasant jangling, of which even the horses were proud, as they often deliberately shook their bells when standing still.

I ought perhaps to have explained that the bell team was usually harnessed tandem fashion, four horses attached to the wagon with trace harness—except for the shaft horse, of course. Their bells are usually stamped with the maker's initials on the inside. There is in Hereford Museum a set of bells used on ox teams, and on a Hampshire farm I saw three 'rumbler' bells, which were much used on packhorses some 150 years ago. These rumblers were also used on the old stage wagons, two per horse. They made no chord, and if all the eight horses had them, the sound must have been heard for miles!

The brasses, worn on brow-band, ear bosses, and martingale, and the plumed flyers, one to three bells, which make a pleasant tinkling but very faint sound, are obviously a survival of the old time bells used for warning traffic.

The origin of all these horse ornaments was the amulet or talisman—a charm worn to ward off evil or misfortune. Today they are more often seen on a wall than on a horse, as it appears to be fashionable to collect horse brasses, and apparently the demand exceeds the supply, as fakes are not unknown.

CHAPTER FIFTEEN

Post-War Coaching

THERE was a time when the coach and four had precedence of all wheeled traffic ; indeed it is recorded, I think of the Dover road, that the driver of His Majesty's Mail claimed precedence over His Majesty's troops and calmly drove through a regiment on the march. That this right of road was something more than a courtesy right seems to be proved by the fact that the military authorities took no action against the driver of the mail.

Such right of road was always claimed (and I always understood it was a legal right) by horsed fire-engines and was continued with the present motorized fire-engines, but a recent case upsets this theory, as apparently they are bound to observe traffic lights.

Up to the 1914-18 war a coach and four still had courtesy precedence, and to a lesser extent, with the growing ignorance of all connected with the horse, up to the late war. Today it appears to me a perilous proceeding to drive four horses. Road manners are almost non-existent towards horsed vehicles and even drivers of mechanical ones are far from courteous to each other. Moreover, the modern police do not understand horse traffic, and are therefore not so helpful as the old bobby, who probably had started his career before the motor entirely usurped the King's highway. Four horses take a lot of wagoning, require plenty of room and a certain amount of time to negotiate corners, etc., and are less easy to manoeuvre than, say, a motor-bus, which takes up about the same amount of floor space. Frequent stops and restarts do not do even a motor engine any good, but it does not tire, whereas stopping and re-starting a heavy vehicle takes it out of horses more than even the length of journey does. Having recently been a passenger on a coach after a gap of some twenty-five years, I think that the modern coachman has far greater difficulties to contend with than any of his predecessors in the various coaching revivals which have at short intervals taken place ever since the real coaching era, which came to an end in the 1840's.

Moreover, modern difficulties are not only those of the road. Apart from crippling taxation and high wages, etc., the food problem is still very difficult for horse-owners, and substitutes for oats are very far from being the same thing. Horses themselves are expensive and few in number, since the horse population steadily decreases year by year. The old Yorkshire coach horse now seems to be extinct, and even the big hackneys, which often took their place in pre-war private drags, seem to have vanished, for I haven't seen any lately. Personally, I always preferred the heavyweight hunter type, but there are not enough to go round for riding, so that not many find their way into harness. Another difficulty is a lack of vehicles. I don't suppose any coach builder has built a coach for at least forty years, so that I was not surprised to hear that the coach I was sitting on was 150 years old. A thing that struck me as curious was that fast-moving motor traffic has apparently put the pedestrian's eye out. Though they are used to keeping well out of the way (jay-walkers excepted), horses trotting at seven or eight miles an hour catch them on the hop. The speed being a good deal quicker than it appears to be, several people had to move faster than they anticipated, including a woman with a perambulator. Traffic lights are equally as disconcerting for the coach driver, for, if they change just as the leaders reach them, the team has to be brought up all standing from the trot with much grinding of brakes. I might add that the smooth surface of modern roads and the absence of grit deprive the brakes of much of their power.

To the man in the street a coaching marathon of seven or eight miles with 60 minutes in which to do it may seem child's play, but under modern conditions the density of traffic alone makes it no easy test of driving, and the constant stopping and starting caused by obstructions, such as automatic traffic signals, combined with hilly roads, with slippery surfaces, make it quite a test of the horses' condition, which is thirty per cent of the points awarded, the marking being : horses thirty per cent ; condition thirty per cent ; coach, harness and equipment forty per cent.

Besides the density of traffic modern road surfaces are unsuited for steel-shod hooves. I was therefore surprised to find a team with neither studs nor pads on their feet, and still more astonished when told they had only once in 1,500 miles had a horse down.

All things considered, it is a very sporting effort to put a coach on the road today, and how few in numbers they are. One particularly misses the Regimental coaches. Even in these mechanized days one still hopes to see the Household Cavalry and Horse Artillery start a coach ; the R.A.S.C. have already done so and given them a lead. I gather one of the greatest difficulties to military sport today is lack of stabling, which in the larger centres has been converted to garages. In fact I have heard of officers being unable to find stabling even for their children's ponies.

To return to post-war coaching, after the 1914-18 war it made a quick recovery. The Remount driven by Mr Walters, being the first on the road followed by Mr Barron, who restarted his Vivid on the Windsor road, and Mr Perkins's coach on the Brighton road. In fact there was soon quite a strong revival. Mr Bertram Mills, Mr Claud Goddard, Mr Colebrook, Mr Hamilton Hughes, and Mr Fred Unwin revived a flickering flame, which died down when Mr Unwin took his coach off the road in 1933. Mr Barron's Venture was, I think, almost the last coach to run out of London ; but even then traffic was so dense that it had to have mounted police help from Piccadilly to Hammersmith.

One used to see classes for these stage coaches as well as for private drags at all the big shows. Alas ! the reduced ranks of the latter are now the sole representatives of a typical British sport. As for road coaches, it is, I am afraid, unlikely that we shall ever see them again. Lack of hotel stabling, grooms and strappers, and lack of horse fodder have, I think, sounded the knell of road coaching, which required much organization, even in the recent past, when conditions were far easier and less expensive than they are today.

To the public a coach today may seem an anachronism, but as it is also a spectacle, its appearance gives obvious pleasure to many onlookers, although some of them evidently vaguely connect it with the films, and the modern driver is apt to be greeted by ribald youths who shout, ' Look out Guvnor ! Dick Turpin's round the corner ! '

How drivers of the present day compare with the past I do not know, since the conditions now are much worse than anything the crack drivers of other days ever had to face. So let us take off our hats to ' a few brave gentlemen putting back the clock '.

CHAPTER SIXTEEN

Off the Ration

THE horse in early times was hunted for food, and the contemporary artists who depicted him on the rocky surface of their caves did so with an accuracy usually lacking in the succeeding and higher civilizations. Probably hunger sharpened the observation of the artist of those days much more often than it has since !

The prehistoric horse as depicted by them was extraordinarily like the Przwalski wild horse of today. Whether this animal still exists in the Gobi desert in a wild state seems open to much doubt, but in captivity some three or four specimens have lingered on. The illustration which appears on page 115 I made at Woburn. This horse—a stallion, apparently sterile—was nineteen years old when I saw it, and I think the last but one of its kind in Britain. Przwalski, a Russian staff officer, discovered this breed of horse in the Gobi Desert, Mongolia, in 1888. In 1900 Hagenbeck of Zoo fame imported twelve yearlings for the Duke of Bedford, seven fillies and five colts (I have seen a photograph of them), and although they bred in captivity they seem to have now died out save this one descendant which I saw in 1948.

Judged by modern equine standards this animal is no beauty, but is none the less interesting. His colour is dun, with no stripe down the back ; buttocks, belly, and chest are white, legs brownish black up to the hocks behind and a little above the knees in front, mane and tail brown. The mane stands up straight and has no forelock. The tail is slightly asinine in type (like a mule's tail). His height I guessed as 13.2 from ten yards range. His voice is definitely the shrill neigh of an entire horse and has no trace of the ass's bray, although in appearance he might well be the missing link between the horse and the ass. His ears are rather large and white, his eyes small and high up in the head, with white round them, and he has a white muzzle, black lips and nostrils, which continue the similarity to the ass. Yet he has four chestnuts like a horse instead of only two on the hind legs like an ass.

52. The Prczwalski wild horse at Woburn Park (1948) with (left) *an Exmoor pony mare.*

I was unable, owing to the long grass, to see his hoofs clearly, but my impression was that he had the narrow box feet of the donkey tribe. He was turned out with two Exmoor ponies slightly smaller than himself, but they apparently were not in foal.

Whether Prczwalski's horse still exists as a wild animal I do not know, but a modern Mongolian horse in a state of more or less pristine purity is still found in the U.S.S.R. (in the Mongolian People's Republic), but according to Victor Kalinin's *Horse Breeding in the Soviet Union* modern hippologists seem rather inclined to the belief that horses of Mongolian origin are more nearly related to the Tarpan, they having only the two chestnuts on hind legs. The Mongolian Tarpan, I might add, has at various times been classified among the asses.

Lydekker's *R. Nat. History,* 1894, describes the Tarpan as reddish grey or dun with a dorsal stripe, large ears bent back, and a convex profile, and a semi-upright mane with a forelock. These animals were also seen by Prczwalski on the steppes. They are classified in most Natural Histories as horses.

The horse population of the U.S.S.R. is said to be immense, and horse-breeding is exceedingly well run by the State. In the most remote primitive districts small horses of Mongolian origin (Altai or Yakub horses) are still used to supply not only transport, but both milk and meat; so that in 1950 we still, like our prehistoric ancestors, depend on the horse

53. The Przewalski wild horse was discovered in Mongolia in 1888. This was the last surviving descendant of twelve imported into England for the Duke of Bedford in 1900.

for food—and not only in the U.S.S.R. Modern mechanical traction has enormously reduced the value of the horse. Our own horse population shrinks at an amazing speed in consequence. You can today travel by car several hundred miles without seeing a mare and foal in the fields. This reduction has been going on for a longish time. I remember fifteen or twenty years ago on Dartmoor being offered a pony mare and foal for a sovereign. They were on their way to the kennels, and a mare and foal being closely akin to a white elephant to a tourist I'm afraid that into the boiler they went. If you go to a farm sale today it is a safe guess that most of the unbroken youngsters and all the unsound working horses will be bought for meat. In fact, it would seem likely that the day is not far off when heavy horses may be bred for meat, and why not? Better that than the extinction of the race.

Those few of us who live among horses hardly realize this decline in our equine population, and those many who do not are never likely to realize it until they see the last survivor in a zoo ! The heaviest reduction is among horses on agricultural holdings, where, in spite of the fact that it has been repeatedly proved that the horse is more economical, the greater speed of the tractor more than neutralizes the greater expense. In 1937 there were 1,004,686 horses engaged in agriculture ; in 1939, 987,415. I have not today's figures, but by 1946 there were 634,000 and in 1947 only 583,000.

According to a recent newspaper article some 500 horses arrive in London every week for slaughter. Another 200 are exported from Ireland to Antwerp, and so it goes on. As only some 16,000 horses are born per annum, this decrease is in no way arrested. I believe there is, or was, a controlled price of £35 for horses for slaughter, and at that the price of a shilling a pound would show a loss. Yet 240 horses per day go to the knacker (I quote from the same source), which means that some 600 tons of horse meat are eaten a week. There would, therefore, appear to be a considerable business in horseflesh, though the number of restaurants displaying a notice that they serve horseflesh is not very great.

I understand that it has been stated there is often a profit of £25 to £70 per horse ! Yet one shilling a pound for human consumption and eightpence for animal consumption could scarcely approach these profits.

According to a Ministry of Agriculture statement, in ten years the horse will be as rare a sight as a hansom cab. It would be a strange irony of fate if Prczwalski's horse, a relic of prehistoric times, should outlast his domesticated successors.

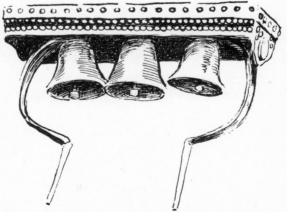

54. *Latten bells with box housing for a shaft horse.*

Index

The numbers in parentheses refer to illustrations